No One
Has Hired Us

BIBLE TRUTHS FOR THE UNEMPLOYED

B. WAYNE BRADFIELD

http://www.bwaynebradfield.com

WESTBOW
P R E S S
A DIVISION OF THOMAS NELSON

Scripture taken from the HOLY BIBLE, NEW INTERNATIONAL VERSION®. Copyright © 1973, 1978, 1984 Biblica. Used by permission of Zondervan. All rights reserved.

WestBow Press books may be ordered through booksellers or by contacting:

WestBow Press
A Division of Thomas Nelson
1663 Liberty Drive
Bloomington, IN 47403
www.westbowpress.com
1-(866) 928-1240

ISBN: 978-1-4497-0943-3 (sc)
ISBN: 978-1-4497-0942-6 (e)

Library of Congress Control Number: 2010941416

Printed in the United States of America

WestBow Press rev. date: 8/24/2011

Contents

INTRODUCTION

Michael K. is a factory worker who has faithfully served the same employer for the past twenty-three years. Today, he learned that the company has been sold to a large corporation that plans to close the plant, resulting in the layoff of all employees.

Susan W. is a single parent who desperately needs a job in order to support her two small children. Restaurants where she once worked are hiring, but the part-time wages are not enough to make ends meet.

Nora J. is a highly qualified research chemist. The firm she has worked for since college has decided to centralize all research, meaning she will be considered redundant.

David P. left high school with a diploma and high hopes. Now—almost one year and many short-term, dead-end jobs later—he is beginning to wonder why he finished school.

Michael, Susan, Nora, and David have at least two things in common: first, they are all in urgent need of suitable employment. Second, all four are sincere, committed Christians.

Does that surprise you? As many devout Christians can testify today, our faith does not provide an automatic insurance policy against unemployment. Sometimes it is just as difficult for the believer to find work as it is for non-believers.

Let me hasten to add the good news, however: Jesus said, "In this world you will have trouble. But take heart! I have overcome the world" (John 16:33). According to the Bible, we too are destined to be overcomers—if we learn to apply God's Word correctly.

Through the study and application of God's Word—the Holy Bible—we can learn to cope with feelings that so often rob us of our peace and lower our effectiveness in taking proper steps to find new employment. Feelings such as shame, guilt, rejection, anger and even despair are fairly normal in such situations, and the Bible addresses each one of these in very clear language. Unfortunately, when Christians display evidence of such feelings, friends sometimes act like Job's "miserable comforters" (Job 16:2, KJV), trying to identify some basic spiritual flaw to explain the situation.

Many excellent books have been written on the subject of how to get a job, and it is not my goal to add another to the library shelves. This study seeks to examine employment and unemployment from a Biblical perspective and will hopefully make suitable companion reading for other self-help books. If the Bible is—as many people say—God's operating manual for successful living, then surely it will be our source of needed wisdom to cope with every life situation, including joblessness.

The title of this study is taken from the parable of the workers in the vineyard, found in Matthew 20:1–19. In that parable, workers were rewarded for their long wait by hearing the words "You also go and work in my vineyard." Thousands upon thousands of people are hoping and praying to hear similar words today. In many cases, the need is desperate.

As neighbors, friends, counselors, or family members of people who become unemployed, what will be our response? What does the Bible say that can provide a word of encouragement or guidance to speak into the life of an unemployed person? Does the Bible have anything to say that is relevant? These types of questions led me on a search that has lasted more than three decades. I am happy to report that God's Word has a great deal to say on the subject.

A Workman Approved by God

In his second letter to the young Timothy, the apostle Paul wrote, "Do your best to present yourself to God as one approved, a workman who does not need to be ashamed and who correctly handles the word of truth" (2 Timothy 2:15). The King James Bible uses the phrase "rightly dividing the word of truth." In the chapters that follow, I have attempted—with God's help—to do that.

Contrary to the opinion of some people, the Bible has great relevance in today's world. I have discovered a virtual gold mine of guidance, instruction, and encouragement for those who would turn to God's Word in times of unemployment. Like gold, however, the nuggets are seldom found on the surface; they must be discovered through some effort. They are found embedded in the principles governing God's kingdom that are scattered throughout the Bible. These principles will not only teach us how we should live, but also how we can make a living.

Because this study involves analysis of God's principles for successful living, there is a constant danger that these will be interpreted as heavenly recipes for material success. Our human minds would like to reduce God to some kind of game show host who would tell us to say the magic word and win the secret prize. That is not how God operates.

According to the writer of Hebrews, "The word of God is living and active. Sharper than any double-edged sword, it penetrates even to dividing soul and spirit, joints and marrow; it judges the thoughts and attitudes of the heart" (Hebrews 4:12). If the Surgeon General were looking for a warning label for the Bible, I believe this quotation would be most suitable.

Studying the Bible can bring radical change to your social habits, your self-image, and your lifestyle. Therefore, if you are perfectly content with the way your life now is, you may want to avoid reading the Bible. However, if you feel a need for change in your life—if you are lacking hope, wisdom, and power in your life and you sincerely want to improve—this study was written with you in mind.

Chapter 1—NO ONE HAS HIRED US

"Why have you been standing here all day long doing nothing?"
They answered, "Because no one has hired us."

This conversation could have been overheard in almost any town or city as recently as yesterday, for we live in a world troubled by unemployment. This particular dialogue, however, is part of a conversation Jesus had with his disciples one day in Judea after speaking with a very wealthy young man. If you have a Bible handy, read the parable of the workers in the vineyard, found at the beginning of Matthew 20. Jesus used that parable to illustrate one of the kingdom principles, but in telling it, he also provided a graphic picture of labor market activity in early Palestine.

People of Jesus' day knew how it felt to be out of work. Wage earners had to compete with slaves and bondsmen for available job opportunities. Agriculture was a main source of employment, and land owners had the option of hiring day laborers for one denarius per day, buying slaves for the equivalent of about seven years' wages, or recruiting bondsmen who would work for room and board.

Many of the people who met Jesus were undoubtedly hoping and praying for work so they could feed their families.

Others were experiencing the injustice of slavery. Oddly enough, I can find no examples in the Bible of Jesus finding jobs for the unemployed, freeing the slaves, or lobbying the governments of the day for laws that would bring about fair employment practices. In fact, on the surface, Jesus appeared to be indifferent where money matters were concerned.

A case in point would be the poor widow who gave all she had (Mark 12:42). Although Jesus spoke highly of her, there is no evidence that he rewarded her with a comfortable income for her faithfulness. Similarly, Jesus demonstrated his ability to feed thousands with only a few loaves and fishes, but there is no record that he ever established soup kitchens or food banks, as we know them today. Instead, he warned his disciples to beware of the yeast (meaning the teaching) of the Pharisees, which would address the needs of the outer man while leaving the inner man destitute (Matthew 16:5–12). Jesus never implied that adequate income and food were not important, but he made it very clear that his followers' priority should be a right relationship with God, whereupon "all these things will be given to you as well" (Matthew 6:33).

We Have Worked All Night

For the unemployed person, perhaps the most encouraging incident recorded in the New Testament is the story of the calling of the first disciples, found in Luke 5:1–11. Jesus borrowed a boat belonging to Simon (later called Peter) and his partners James and John, intending to use it as a kind of podium in order to speak to a large crowd of people. After speaking to the crowd, Jesus instructed Peter to put out into deep water and let down the nets. Remember, these men were professionals, highly skilled in the art of catching fish and well aware of the feeding habits, and usual habitats of commercially viable species. Just like you and me, these fishermen worked to feed their families and pay the bills. Notice that Jesus did not ask Peter to do this in order to "try his luck," or to see what would happen. He was very specific about the expected result—if Peter obeyed.

Simon Peter replied, "Master, we have worked all night and haven't caught anything." Those words were undoubtedly spoken out of frustration and, perhaps, some discouragement as Peter faced the prospect of telling his family the disappointing result of his night's work. But Peter was no fool. He knew there was something very authentic about Jesus, a man who talked about God with an authority unequalled by any other teacher of the day. And so, Peter quickly added, "But because you say so, I will let down the nets." According to the Scripture, it took two boats to bring the resulting catch to shore. This miracle literally not only drove Peter to his knees and to repentance, but also caused all three of the partners to realize that Jesus could and would supply all of their needs *if they would only follow him*.

Your Heavenly Father Knows

In Matthew 6:25–34, Jesus provided a detailed picture of a loving heavenly Father who knows, not only our every need, but also the needs of all of nature. According to Jesus, if God feeds and clothes the birds of the air and the flowers of the field, how much more will he feed and clothe his children?

The first and the best reason why we should study God's Word in relation to finding a job, then, is to learn and understand the basic principles that apply to God's plan for meeting our needs. The Psalmist sang to God, "Your word is a lamp to my feet and a light for my path" (Psalm 119:105). I don't know about you, but when I'm faced with problems that seem beyond my comprehension and worries that threaten to overpower me, I don't often know which way to turn. I've discovered, however, that God knows my every need, and has provided his Word to light my path and direct my feet in times of trouble.

Wisdom that Has Been Hidden

In the second chapter of his first letter to the Corinthian church, the apostle Paul wrote about God's secret wisdom, which was hidden from the rulers of the age. This hidden wisdom came from the Spirit of God and was and is understood only by those who receive God's Spirit. Without the discernment of the Spirit, God's wisdom is said to appear as foolishness to the world (1 Corinthians 2:14).

This is the second reason why we need to turn to the Word of God when faced with the problem of unemployment. The Bible tells us how to receive God's Spirit. Doing so leads us to the deeper things of God. Care must be exercised, however, that we don't view Christianity as some mystic society holding wisdom and understanding under lock and key, lest they be misused. On the contrary, keys that will open the door to these blessings are offered freely to all who will receive God's Spirit.

How do we receive God's Spirit? Romans 8:14 says that those who are led by the Spirit of God are the children of God. John 1:12 tells us how to become the children of God: "to all who receive him [Jesus], and believe in his name, he gave the right to become the children of God." If we will only choose to receive the gift of salvation, paid for by the sacrifice of Jesus on the cross, God has promised to give us his Holy Spirit. It is this same Holy Spirit who enables us to believe on the name of Jesus and to understand the mysteries of God's wisdom.

If you have never received Jesus as your personal Saviour, I invite you to do that now, "so that your faith might not rest on men's wisdom, but on God's power" (1 Corinthians 2:5). Simply bow your head right now and ask the Father to show you how you should pray, confessing your need for forgiveness and inviting Jesus to come into your life.

If you have taken this step for the first time, take a moment now and write the date, time, and circumstances in a safe place (such as the inside cover of your Bible). If you don't have a Bible, get one right away and begin to read it daily. I can promise without hesitation that this will be a "red letter day" in your life as you reflect on it in the future. The Bible says that you have just become a new creation, adopted into God's family. You have become a joint heir with Jesus (2 Corinthians 5:17, Romans 8:17). Congratulations!

Peter describes your experience this way: "Praise be to the God and Father of our Lord Jesus Christ! In his great mercy he has given us new birth into a living hope through the resurrection of Jesus Christ from the dead, and into an inheritance that can never perish, spoil or fade—kept in heaven for you" (1 Peter 1:3, 4).

Hope as an Anchor

In Ephesians 1:18–19, the apostle Paul expresses three wishes for the young Christians in Ephesus—three things he is praying that they will come to know. The first of these is the "hope to which he has called you." Verses 13 and 14 of the same chapter provide an explanation of this hope: "Having believed, you were marked in him with a seal, the promised Holy Spirit, who is a deposit guaranteeing our inheritance until the redemption of those who are God's possession."

When we first believe in Christ, Paul says that God gives us a deposit, or down payment of his Holy Spirit. The first task of the Holy Spirit is to assure the new believer that he or she has come into an inheritance as one of God's possessions. That inheritance includes a new home in heaven to be claimed on the day of our redemption. Often, the first and most convincing sign to a new believer that Jesus has really entered his or her life is a new hope for eternal life. People find it difficult to put into words, but somehow they know that if they were to die tonight, a home is waiting for them in heaven. No matter how difficult times may be or how stormy the seas of life may get, "we have this hope as an anchor for the soul, firm and secure" (Hebrews 6:19).

But hope does not stop at the promise of eternal life with Jesus. Hope also makes a profound difference in our day-to-day walk, especially when we face problems like unemployment. Of all the tools of destruction wielded by the devil, I believe the spirit of hopelessness is perhaps the most prevalent, causing untold misery to rich and poor alike. It is not hard to understand why people in third world countries would be plagued by hopelessness, but we might be surprised to learn just how many people in affluent societies have the same spirit. Having everything to live *with,* but nothing to live *for,* people are trying to give meaning to life in the accumulation of possessions and the pursuit of diversions. In a desperate attempt to find meaning in life, many are reaching out to false religions and humanistic philosophies, which only compound their confusion. The answer to hopelessness is Jesus. He alone can restore purpose and meaning to our lives.

I cannot think of God's precious gift of hope without recalling an illustration that I read as a young man. It has had a profound effect on my life. A former World War II navy chaplain told of being assigned to a U.S. ship that saw fierce combat in the battle for the Philippine Islands. Late in the war, while docked in Manila, the captain of the ship received orders to return to the United States. The announcement of their new destination brought shouts of joy from the battle-weary crew. All over the ship, sailors were heard to tell each other time and again, "We're going home! We're going home!"

As the ship steamed past Corregidor and Bataan, there were brief periods of sadness as the crew recalled the many servicemen who had given their lives on the beaches—but then their thoughts turned eastward. "We're going home!" Despite enemy aircraft sightings, two weeks of heavy storms at sea, and the constant diet of dehydrated eggs and potatoes, spirits remained high among the crew. "We're going home!" That is the same hope that keeps us going when life's problems seem overwhelming. No matter how difficult our present circumstances, we can agree with the old hymn: "We have an anchor that keeps the soul, steadfast and sure while the billows roll." *We're going home!*

The Riches of God's Grace

Paul's second prayer for the Ephesians was that they would know God's riches. The apostle frequently mentioned God's riches in his writings, but he was not referring to money or possessions. We live in a world full of contradictions. We give great praise and large salaries to those who look and perform best in their chosen field, whether in sports, entertainment, or commerce. We idolize and try to imitate those who accumulate great wealth and possessions. But the Bible tells us that God is not greatly impressed by our popularity, position, or even our bank accounts.

Consider the story of the rich man who asked Jesus, "What shall I do to inherit eternal life?" (Luke 18:18–27) Realizing that this man valued his wealth more than God himself, Jesus advised him to go, sell everything, and give his money to the poor. Jesus had nothing against prosperity. Some of his friends were wealthy, and there is no evidence that he gave similar advice to them. He did, however, emphasize repeatedly that God is much more interested in the condition of our hearts than in the thickness of our wallets.

True riches, according to Paul, are a product of God's grace, which he has "lavished on us with all wisdom and understanding" (Ephesians 1:7–8). These riches come to us through Christ, "in whom are hidden all the treasures of wisdom and knowledge" (Colossians 2:3). The genuine riches of God consist of his wisdom, his understanding, and his knowledge. We will examine this topic more deeply in a later chapter, but in the meantime, it is important for us to recognize that God has made provisions for us to receive and experience his brand of riches in every situation, including unemployment.

Just think about that! If you can gain the wisdom, knowledge, and understanding of the God who created the universe, how can you fail to succeed?

His Incomparably Great Power

This was Paul's third prayer for us. If there is one life situation that can make a person feel powerless, it is the lack of work. One day we are secure in a good job, and then the rug is pulled out from underneath us and we join the ranks of the unemployed. At times like this, we need to know that God brings his power into our lives. Paul said, "I pray also that the eyes of your heart may be enlightened in order that you may know—his incomparably great power for us who believe. That power is like the working of his mighty strength, which he exerted in Christ when he raised him from the dead and seated him at his right hand in the heavenly realms, far above all rule and authority, power and dominion, and every title that can be given, not only in the present age but also in the one to come" (Ephesians 1:18–21).

Of all the gifts we receive from the Father, this is perhaps the most difficult one to understand. The Greek word used often in the New Testament to denote power is the word from which we get the English word *dynamite*. Just like dynamite, God's power in our lives needs to be handled with care. Many people of Jesus' day had trouble in this area. They were looking for a man who would be "the lion to the tribe of Judah" (Hosea 5:14), who would tear evil leaders apart and establish a new kingdom on earth. Instead, God sent Jesus, whom John described as a "Lamb who was slain to receive power" (Revelation 5:12). Isaiah had prophesied about this, saying, "He was led like a lamb to the slaughter. Therefore I will give him a portion among the great, and he will divide the spoils with the strong, because he poured out his life unto death" (Isaiah 53:7, 12).

Following his death and resurrection, Christ appeared to his followers and declared, "you will receive power when the Holy Spirit comes on you; and you will be my witnesses" (Acts 1:8). God's power is always linked directly to our Christian witness. He will manifest his power in our lives in order to provide a testimony of his love and his grace so that we might be overcomers and so that others may see and believe. Trouble will come to believers and non-believers alike in this world, but through the resurrection power of Jesus Christ, God wants to use the faith of his children to show everyone the way to victory over every situation.

The hope that Jesus has placed in our hearts will enable us to rest in him, no matter what the world tries to do to us. His riches of wisdom, understanding, and knowledge will enable us to see beyond our current circumstances and make right choices during these periods of upheaval in our lives. And if we are willing, his quiet power will begin to transform us from the inside out, until we can honestly say with the apostle, "I have learned the secret of being content in any and every situation, whether well fed or hungry, whether living in plenty or in want. I can do everything through him who gives me strength" (Philippians 4:12–13).

Life Application—Chapter 1

It is clear that God wants to meet our needs, but his provision is not always automatic. In your own words, what does the Bible have to say about God's provision, and how we can receive it? Begin with the following verses, and then search the Bible for additional examples and instructions on this topic. As you read through the remaining chapters of this study, you may discover a few more lines which you can add to this list, so leave some space in your notes for additional Bible references and comments.

Psalm 128:1–2

Proverbs 11:25

Isaiah 45:7

Luke 6:38

2 Corinthians 9:6–11

Chapter 2—BREAD OF ADVERSITY

Why me? What did I do to deserve this? What am I supposed to do now? How will I be able to support my family?

These questions—and many more—come flooding into the mind of the person who has just lost a job. Depending on our circumstances and personalities, we may react with anger, fear, shame, self-pity, or any combination of the above. There is a strong temptation to feel singled out and rejected by those whom we trusted. Bitterness and resentment may surface as we struggle with feelings of anger toward those who had the power to send us into unemployment.

Just at the time when our minds are overwhelmed with all of this extra baggage, the world expects us to begin making rational decisions that will affect our whole future. *Do I need a resume? Should I visit an agency? Do I need to look into retraining? Should I start my own business? Where do I begin?* And for the Christian, there is an added dimension: *Where does God fit into all of this confusion? If God really loves me, as his Bible teaches, why am I going through this? Why did God not intervene to allow me to keep my job?* Some people confess to being angry toward God. This anger is brought on by a feeling of rejection or even persecution.

At times like these, we need to seek help. This is not a time to be proud and independent. In many communities, there are counselors who have been trained to help people become employed. In almost every public library, there are books that can provide similar counsel. These sources are invaluable for conducting a successful job search and should be used liberally by every unemployed worker.

The best help of all, however, is found through reading the Bible. Listen to what God said through the prophet Isaiah: "Although the Lord gives you the bread of adversity and the water of affliction, your teachers will be hidden no more; with your own eyes you will see them. Whether you turn to the right or to the left, your ears will hear a voice behind you, saying, 'This is the way; walk in it'" (Isaiah 30:20–21). Hundreds of years before the apostle Paul wrote to the church at Corinth about God's hidden wisdom, the prophet Isaiah wrote to the followers of God in Jerusalem about exactly the same thing! The fact is that God has provided us with a complete book of instructions, covering every possible life situation. He has given the Holy Spirit as both teacher and comforter, and he has promised never to leave us or forsake us. What more can we ask?

God is Treating You as Sons

"Why me?" we ask. The world will offer a variety of reasons why we find ourselves unemployed: economic conditions, technical change, industrial restructuring, increased foreign competition … the list goes on and on. The Bible has a tendency to bring everything down to a very personal level, however—and sometimes we really don't want to hear what it has to say.

Isaiah says that it is the Lord himself who gives us the bread of adversity. We thought it was the world, or perhaps it was the devil himself. One of the most often quoted verses from the book of Job is, "The Lord gave and the Lord has taken away" (Job 1:21). Notice that the Scripture does not say that the Lord gave and the devil has taken away. Why would God allow adversity or hardship in our lives and even take back some of the good things he has given us? The writer of Hebrews tells us, "God is treating you as sons. For what son is not disciplined by his father?" (Hebrews 12:7) Take heart, however, for our Lord Jesus Christ himself endured even greater discipline from his Father. Speaking of Jesus, the same writer says, "Even though he was a son, he learned obedience from what he suffered" (Hebrews 5:8).

Notice that in the Bible, discipline is always linked to a learning process. The Psalmist says, "it was good for me to be afflicted, so that I might learn your decrees" (Psalm 119:73). When we face difficulties, we get serious about finding a solution. The benefits of our learning in these situations are directed both inward and outward. James says, "Consider it pure joy, my brothers, whenever you face trials of many kinds, because you know that the testing of your faith develops perseverance. Perseverance must finish its work so that you may be mature and complete, not lacking in anything" (James 1:2–4). Take note that it is our faith that is being tested and not our strength, and that maturity will be the result—to the point where we will not be lacking in anything.

Every father has great plans for his sons and daughters, and God is no different. In the final analysis, God has two plans that apply to everyone who is born of the Spirit. First, he would have us continually "being transformed into his [Jesus'] likeness with ever increasing glory" (2 Corinthians 3:18, see also Romans 8:29). As we allow the fruit of the Spirit—i.e., "love, joy, peace, patience, kindness, goodness, faithfulness, gentleness and self-control" (Galatians 5:22–23)—to grow in our lives, we become more like Jesus. No doubt this process is preparing us for our eventual home in heaven, where we will be "like him" (1 John 3:2); it also allows others to see Jesus in us right now.

God's second plan for all of his children is that they should be doing the work of Jesus. Jesus himself said, "anyone who has faith in me will do what I have been doing. He will do even greater things than these, because I am going to the Father" (John 14:12). Read the full context of this statement of Jesus, and it becomes abundantly clear that today's believers, who are called the body of Christ, should be continuing the full ministry that Christ had when he walked on earth. We can only do that through the power of the Holy Spirit as we move in unity of the Spirit and allow the gifts of the Spirit to flow through us as outlined in 1 Corinthians 12–14.

This does not mean that we are all to become preachers, evangelists, or missionaries; it does mean that no matter what our calling or occupation may be, these two fundamental plans of God apply directly to all believers.

The Lord Is My Shepherd

Jesus said, "I am the good shepherd; I know my sheep and my sheep know me" (John 10:14). Most of us know the Psalm that begins, "The Lord is my Shepherd, I shall not want" (Psalm 23:1). Many years before Jesus was born, the prophet Micah had foretold the birth of Jesus, saying, "He will stand and shepherd his flock in the strength of the Lord, in the majesty of the name of the Lord his God" (Micah 5:4). Later Micah added this word of instruction: "Shepherd your people with your staff, the flock of your inheritance" (Micah 7:14). We know that a shepherd carries his staff for many reasons, not the least of which is to guide the wandering lambs away from danger by placing the hooked end around the animal's neck. Likewise, our Father—our good shepherd—will sometimes provide firm guidance when we are prone to wander.

When bad things happen to us—such as a sudden layoff or a business failure—we often wonder where God is in all of this disappointment and despair. We may feel abandoned by God and Jesus, when the truth is that God is only being a father, and Jesus is still our shepherd. As we study God's Word, we read of many times when God allowed his people to pass through difficult times in order to lead and guide them into a better way. Our response should be to dig deeper into the Word of God in order to quickly learn what he would have us know.

Just like the early disciples, we sometimes have to learn the hard way—through experience. We may encounter temporary interruptions in our orderly lives, as the Lord "pours us out into new vessels" in order to leave behind habits and activities that are not good for us (Jeremiah 48:11). We may even experience hard times, as God allows his "refiner's fire" to burn away impurities and harmful desires from our hearts (Malachi 3:2). All of us from time to time will experience the cutting edge of God's pruning shears, as he grooms and prepares us for our destiny (John 15:2). Farmers know very well that many fruit and vegetable plants have a tendency to grow what they call "suckers"—fast growing and largely unproductive shoots emanating from the main stalk or branches. Such unwanted growth tends to draw away nourishment that is needed by the legitimate branches of the plant. If allowed to remain, the suckers will cause a reduction in the size and quality of the crop. Just like those plants, we all are tempted to branch off into activities and diversions that are unproductive—and even harmful—to our purpose in life.

But God is a gentle father who will tactfully point out our need for change as we read his Word and commune with him in prayer. When we refuse to respond to his quiet nudging or neglect to attend to his Word and prayer, then we become prime candidates for the more radical corrections. "A fool spurns his father's discipline, but whoever heeds correction shows prudence" (Proverbs 15:5).

Almost every major character mentioned in the Bible had to undergo periods of drought, famine, persecution, or failure of some kind. Believing in God does not provide us with an automatic immunity to suffering—but through our faith, God will use these hard times to grow and shape us to be the sons and daughters that he planned before the beginning of time. Faith in God will not guarantee that your life will always be easy. Trials will come to everyone, because we live in an imperfect world. But as many wise men and women have pointed out, it is not our difficulties that set us apart, but how we respond and act in the face of those difficulties. God desires to show us how to face and go through our difficult times—by simply trusting in his Word.

After the death of Moses, Joshua was chosen by God to lead the Hebrew nation into the Promised Land. This was no easy task, but God made a pledge to Joshua that he would be with him, on one condition: "Do not let this Book of the Law depart from your mouth; meditate on it day and night, so that you may be careful to do everything written in it. *Then you will be prosperous and successful*" (Joshua 1:8, emphasis added).

The Desires of Your Heart

The Scriptures say, "Delight yourself in the Lord and he will give you the desires of your heart. Commit your way to the Lord; trust in him and he will do this" (Psalm 37:3–4). Some well-meaning Christians use this scripture verse to imply that God will give us everything we want if we trust in him. If that interpretation were correct, then we would have thousands more evangelists with the world impact of Billy Graham, and Bill Gates would have to compete with hundreds and thousands of people for his title as one of the world's richest men. But God is not promising to always give us the *object* of every desire we feel. The truth is that God *places in us* those desires that will motivate and sustain us as we carry out his will for our lives. Our God-breathed desires will always line up perfectly with the work that the Father has planned for our life, and they can point us to that work if we will only take time to examine the very heart that God has placed in us. It follows, then, that we should do everything possible to identify those desires that God wants to place in our hearts.

Look again at Psalm 37:

1. Delight yourself in the Lord.
2. Commit your way to the Lord.
3. Trust in the Lord.

The first condition is, "Delight yourself in the Lord." The word *delight* means "to enjoy or take pleasure in something or someone". God really wants his children to enjoy their relationship with him. He wants us to take great pleasure in the reading and study of his Word. When we do that, we begin to get a new appreciation for his Spirit within us. Two of the Hebrew root words for the term *delight* are "soft" and "pliable". As we mature in our faith, our relationship with God goes well beyond mere enjoyment, and we find ourselves the subjects of a heart transplant given by the Holy Ghost—we desire fervently to do his will in every area of our lives.

The second condition is "Commit your way to the Lord." One of the synonyms for the word *commit* is "hand over," which means "to surrender." God wants Jesus to be Lord, controlling every area of our lives—but our human nature also strives for control. The battleground is our soul, and it is made up of our mind, will, and emotions. This battle cannot be taken lightly. That is why the apostle Paul wrote, "work out your salvation with fear and trembling" (Philippians 2:12). If you read the verses preceding that statement in Philippians, Paul is pleading with us to make Jesus the absolute Lord of our lives. He is referring to the deliverance of our mind, will, and emotions from the control of the flesh. "Put to death, therefore, whatever belongs to your earthly nature" (Colossians 3:5). Give Jesus full control.

The third condition is to trust in the Lord. Proverbs 3:5–6 reads "Trust in the Lord with all your heart and lean not on your own understanding; in all your ways acknowledge him, and he will make your paths straight." In very simple terms, trust is faith in action. I can have great faith in the safety of the balcony just outside the window where this page is being written, but that faith means very little if I am not willing to trust the builders of the balcony and step out onto it. Believing is important, but it must lead to trusting, which requires an outward act of commitment.

The psalmist, David, clearly understood the relationship between our obedience to God's Word and our ability to succeed in life: "Blessed is the man who does not walk in the counsel of the wicked or stand in the way of sinners or sit in the seat of mockers. But his delight is in the law of the Lord, and on his law he meditates day and night. He is like a tree planted by streams of water, which yields its fruit in season and whose leaf does not wither. Whatever he does prospers." (Psalm 1:1–3).

Even David had to learn that success does not happen overnight, but that it is a product of our willingness to be planted near the river of God's Word and our patience to wait for the season when we see the fruit of our faithfulness. Every tree is tested by the winds of life, and those that survive are the trees that have put their roots deep into the soil. Even in periods of severe drought, that tree will not see its leaves wither, because it is planted next to the streams of water. And in its season, that tree will bear good fruit.

If you are like that tree, God's Word says that whatever you do will prosper.

Life Application—Chapter 2

The Bible lists a number of reasons for and benefits of the troubles that we encounter as believers. Look up the following scriptures, and note what the Word says about cause and effect:

1. Adversity: Literally meaning a "tight place" in the Hebrew, this word also carried the connotation of having an adversary or enemy. Note what the following verses say:

1 Peter 5:8–10

Proverbs 17:17

James 1:2–4

2. Affliction: The Hebrew word used here is derived from a word meaning "to press," and alternate interpretations can be to "distress, crush, force, hold fast or oppress."

Isaiah 48:10

Psalm 119:92–93

3. Trials: The Greek word used by James (James 1:2) means literally "a putting to proof." How many times have we used the term "tried and true"?

Hebrews 12:4–14

1 Peter 1:6–7

Chapter 3—TRUE RICHES

While working in supervision and management, I had opportunities to participate in a number of training courses that focused on the art of managing human enterprise. People love to theorize, categorize, and prioritize every aspect of human endeavors, hoping to discover the formula that will lead to success. For that reason, we have seen a host of management strategies come and go, each of which has been introduced as an improvement over those of the past. But as I participated in all of these studies, I had a growing sense that we were only addressing the surface issues. We were getting better at defining and labelling the problems, which then allowed us to plan and organize our work more effectively. But the underlying, pivotal keys to success or failure were being overlooked.

Then to my surprise, I discovered that the best management strategy of all is written in the Bible. God had it there all the time—but because of its simplicity, I tended to read right past it. Turn to Proverbs 24:3–4:

> "By wisdom, a house is built,
>   and through understanding it is established;
> through knowledge its rooms are filled
>   with rare and beautiful treasures."

These verses are paraphrased in *The Living Bible* as follows: "Any enterprise is built by wise planning, becomes strong through common sense, and profits wonderfully by keeping abreast of the facts." As noted in Chapter 1, wisdom, understanding, and knowledge are three examples of the riches we can receive from God.

It is interesting that these three attributes—wisdom, understanding, and knowledge—are included in the list of seven spirits that Isaiah prophesied would accompany the coming Messiah (Isaiah 11:2). I believe that these are the same seven spirits which we will someday see standing before the throne of God (Revelation 1:4). The first is the Spirit of the Lord, accompanied by the spirits of wisdom, understanding, counsel, power, knowledge, and fear of the Lord. These same seven spirits were foreshadowed by the seven lamps that stood in the Holy Place of the Tabernacle (Exodus 25:37). Just as the seven lamps provided light to guide the priests toward the Most Holy Place, the seven spirits point us to the very heart of God. They represent spiritual light, and John calls them the "seven spirits of God" (Revelation 4:5). God's light is pure, unchanging, and without any shadows or variations. James describes it this way: "Every good and perfect gift is from above, coming down *from the Father of the heavenly lights,* who does not change like shifting shadows" (James 1:17, emphasis added). According to the vision given to Zechariah, the seven lamps are "the eyes of the Lord, which range throughout the earth" (Zechariah 4:10b). In 2 Chronicles 16:9, we read that "the eyes of the Lord range throughout the earth *to strengthen* those whose hearts are fully committed to him" (emphasis added).

Would you like to be strengthened by God? Would you like to see each situation that you face through the eyes of God? Would you like to have more wisdom, better understanding, and the necessary knowledge to cope with the problems of life? If your answer is yes, then I have good news for you. According to 2 Peter 1:3, "His divine power has given us *everything we need* for life and godliness, through our knowledge of him who called us by his own glory and goodness" (emphasis added). Note the past tense: God *has already given* us everything necessary for victory and holiness!

When we receive Jesus and make him our Lord, he brings with him all of the attributes that we need in order to live life victoriously. As we get to know Jesus through Bible study, prayer, and meditation, we will begin to experience the energy of his Holy Spirit, bringing light into our minds and spirits. Scripture verses which once seemed dead and lifeless suddenly jump off the pages to bring an awesome revelation of God's truth and love. Just as the bowl in Zechariah's vision provided oil to energize the seven lamps, the oil of God's Holy Spirit fuels a virtual explosion of God's kingdom principles which speak directly to our life situations. This fact alone should be reason enough for anyone who is honestly seeking the true meaning of life to *run* to the nearest church where the words of the Bible are treated as the inerrant words of God, our father.

As I pondered the words of Paul regarding the mystery of God's riches, I found myself wondering why he would single out only three of the seven spirits to represent God's riches for his people. What is there that sets wisdom, understanding, and knowledge apart from the other four spirits? My attention was drawn to Proverbs 3:19–20: "By wisdom the Lord laid the earth's foundations, by understanding he set the heavens in place; by his knowledge the deeps were divided, and the clouds let drop the dew." I believe that these two verses hold the key: wisdom, understanding, and knowledge are the tools that God used to create the universe, and therefore it follows that these are the attributes which we should pursue vigorously in order to succeed in the construction of our lives. Knowing this, God's theory of management expressed in Proverbs 24:3–4 takes on great importance. If God uses wisdom, understanding, and knowledge in the act of creation, how much more should we who are created in his image use the same attributes to manage our lives, our families, and our careers?

Wisdom is Supreme

In Proverbs 4:7, we read, "Wisdom is supreme; therefore get wisdom." To my knowledge, there are no universities that list "Wisdom 101" as a course of studies. They do teach philosophy, which involves the intellectual pursuit of wisdom, but true wisdom does not reside in the human intellect. True wisdom resides in our spirit and is a gift of God. James says, "If any of you lacks wisdom, he should ask God, who gives generously to all without finding fault, and it will be given to him" (James 1:5). According to Psalm 111:10 and Proverbs 9:10, "the fear of the Lord is the beginning of wisdom." In the simplest terms I can think of, the wise person knows the difference between right and wrong from God's perspective, is keenly aware of the consequences of wrong choices, and chooses the good and acceptable path in all situations.

It is not enough to simply know what is right and wrong, but our greatest challenge is to apply that knowledge to every decision we make based on our understanding of the consequences, and motivated by an intense desire to please God. Like happiness, wisdom is not a station that we arrive at, but rather a way of travelling. To learn more about the critical importance of wisdom in your life, read one chapter in the book of Proverbs every day.

Get Understanding

Proverbs 4:5 tells us to "get understanding." When we pass through periods of tribulation such as unemployment, we struggle to understand the *why* of our situation. We know only too well *what* is going on, but it is the *why* that causes a whole host of emotional reactions in us. We cannot see any good reason for what is occurring, and that gives rise to fear, anger, self-doubt, and even depression. Relationships often become strained as we react to these feelings that seem to be out of control. We feel that we could correct the situation if only we could understand why we were chosen to pass through this ordeal, but our lack of understanding makes us feel completely powerless. It just does not seem fair!

In the midst of his great tribulation, Job cried out, "where does understanding dwell?" (Job 28:20) Then in Job 28:23, he came to the realization that God "understands the way to it, and he alone knows where it dwells." Solomon said "knowledge of the Holy One is understanding" (Proverbs 9:10). It is important for us to realize that true understanding—just like true wisdom—comes from the Spirit of God through Jesus, our Lord. That is surely why the Scripture tells us to "Trust in the Lord with all your heart, and lean not on your own understanding" (Proverbs 3:5).

In Old Testament times, the Spirit of God was not available to the average believer, but it rested on God's anointed servants. Psalm 103:7 reads: "He made known his ways to Moses, his deeds to the people of Israel." Thankfully, God did not leave mankind in that state. Before Jesus left to be with the Father, he promised to send a comforter—the Holy Spirit—to come and dwell with all of those who would receive his free gift of salvation. Furthermore, he declared that this same Holy Spirit would lead believers into all truth. I don't know about you, but I want to understand more than just the deeds of God—and thanks to the availability of the Holy Spirit, it is now within our grasp to understand many of God's ways. The portion of understanding that we need and can accept will be provided through God's Spirit, causing us to grow in the knowledge of God's ways. Therefore, get understanding. Ask God, and he will answer.

Keep in mind that God does not promise complete understanding to us here on earth. Deuteronomy 29:29 says:

"The secret things belong to the Lord our God, but the things revealed belong to us and to our children forever, that we may follow all the words of this law". Perhaps we will be able to understand everything when we reach heaven.

Knowledge of the Truth

Unless you have been living on another planet recently, you know that our world has been experiencing a virtual explosion in the growth of knowledge. The phenomenal growth of computers has provided instant access to huge amounts of information by almost anyone. The term "information overload" has taken on new meaning. For the unemployed person who is facing the possibility of having to learn a new trade or profession, the so-called "information age" brings a whole new set of problems related to job-hunting. Many of the people now being laid off are victims of new technology as employers reduce payroll costs in order to justify heavy investments in manufacturing and information technology. Many workers have been innocent bystanders while investment companies buy, sell, trade, merge, and relocate world-class companies that were considered hometown institutions until recently. A whole new batch of terminology has emerged that is aimed at softening the blow of large-scale human manipulation in the pursuit of the bottom line. Words like "downsizing" and "out placing" are examples. No matter what we call it, unemployment is still unemployment, and it can be devastating for many who experience it.

From a Biblical perspective, I believe that this period of time could be called the age of misinformation. Never in the history of mankind has there been so much information generated that is either exaggerated, half-true, or altogether untrue. In 2 Timothy 4:3–4, Paul writes this about the last days: "For the time will come when men will not put up with sound doctrine. Instead, to suit their own desires, they will gather around them a great number of teachers to say what their itching ears want to hear. They will turn their ears away from the truth and turn aside to myths." God help us! I believe that the time Paul talked about has arrived.

Take a stroll down the main street of almost any large city today and see if you don't agree with the prophet Isaiah when he declared, "truth has stumbled in the streets, honesty cannot enter. Truth is nowhere to be found, and whoever shuns evil becomes a prey" (Isaiah 59:14b, 15a).

Turn on your television set or your computer this evening and see if God's words spoken through the prophet Jeremiah are not coming true once more: "Friend deceives friend, and no one speaks the truth. They have taught their tongues to lie; they weary themselves with sinning. You live in the midst of deception; in their deceit they refuse to acknowledge me, declares the Lord" (Jeremiah 9:5–6). I believe you will agree that most behavior and attitudes portrayed on television and movie screens today are threatening to destroy the morals, minds, and will of this entire generation. Our computers now have brought new opportunities to fill our eyes and minds with misinformation. Blogging and social networking have opened a virtual floodgate of verbal criticism and abuse of anyone who would advocate Christian morals.

Allow me to make one dare! I dare you to print or copy the words of Psalm 101 and place them near your television remote and your mouse pad. Then read the psalm thoughtfully as a pledge to God each time you tune in or log on. See if these words will not have a huge impact on what you watch. Psalm 101 could well be entitled "God's TV Guide":

> I will set before my eyes no vile thing.
> The deeds of faithless men I hate; they will not cling to me.
> Men of perverse heart shall be far from me; I will have nothing to do with evil.

> Whoever slanders his neighbor in secret, him will I
> put to silence;
> Whoever has haughty eyes and a proud heart, him
> will I not endure.
> My eyes will be on the faithful in the land, that they
> may dwell with me;
> He whose walk is blameless will minister to me.
> No one who practices deceit will dwell in my house;
> No one who speaks falsely will stand in my
> presence.
> Every morning I will put to silence all the wicked in the
> land;
> I will cut off every evildoer from the city of the Lord
> (Psalm 101:3–8).

You may memorize enough information to answer every trivial pursuit question ever dreamed up, but if you don't have discernment of God's truth, your knowledge remains just that—information. Every field of human endeavor now has its information brokers—people who have gathered, categorized, and offered to sell or trade their information as a commodity. Our libraries, computer banks, and even our brains are filled with information that may be accurate, but it would be misleading to call much of it the knowledge of truth.

God's Word is truth. Jesus declared that he is "the Way, the Truth, and the Life" (John 14:6), and the Holy Spirit has come in order to lead believers into "all truth" (John 16:13). When we receive God's riches of wisdom and understanding, we will begin to discern what is true and what is false. Using the Bible as our standard, we will be able to test information reaching our eyes and ears against the truth and wisdom of all of God's anointed teachers, including Moses, David, Solomon, and Jesus. In addition, the Holy Spirit will begin to warn us through our own spirit when false information is being conveyed. As we study the Scriptures and grow in our Christian walk, this ability to discern the truth will increase.

God will even bring to our minds the knowledge we need to win the job he has planned for us. To his disciples, Jesus said: "When you are brought before … authorities, do not worry about how you will defend yourselves or what you will say, for the Holy Spirit will teach you at that time what you should say" (Luke 12:11–12). Jesus would say the same thing to today's Christian job-hunters. When we walk into a room where we will be interviewed for the job that God has set aside for us, the Holy Spirit will attend the interview, guiding and directing the words that we say. This does not excuse us from studying and knowing what products or services the employer provides or from ensuring that we have seriously considered how our experience, skills, and abilities relate to the position at hand. But the Holy Spirit will bring to our minds the appropriate words in order to showcase our potential worth to the employer in ways that we could never accomplish alone.

Today, millions of people are investing heavily in higher education, hoping to obtain the wisdom, understanding, and knowledge that will lead to a successful career. Most have never heard that the greatest wisdom, the most profound understanding, and the knowledge of truth are not found in textbooks, but that they are part of the spiritual gifting that God has for those who would approach him in spirit and in truth. Pray that God will give you his wisdom, his understanding, and his knowledge.

Life Application—Chapter 3

The Word of God gives specific methods for receiving the wisdom, understanding and knowledge of God. Study the following verses, and jot down the advice contained in each one.

1. Getting Wisdom

Deuteronomy 34:9

1 Kings 4:29–30

2 Chronicles 1:12

Proverbs 1:1–2

Ecclesiastes 2:26

Luke 21:15

1 Corinthians 2:13

2. Getting Understanding

1 Kings 4:29

Psalm 111:10

Daniel 1:17

Ephesians 1:7–10

Colossians 2:2–3

1 John 5:20

3. Getting Knowledge

1 Timothy 2:3–4

Psalm 119:66

Proverbs 2:1–5

1 Corinthians 1:5–6

2 Peter 1:5–8

Chapter 4—BE THOROUGHLY EQUIPPED

"All Scripture is God-breathed and useful for teaching, rebuking, correcting and training in righteousness, so that the man of God may be thoroughly equipped for every good work" (2 Timothy 3:16–17).

Long before we were born, God had a purpose and a plan for our lives. Just as most earthly fathers have dreams and hopes for their sons and daughters, our Heavenly Father cares deeply about our success and happiness. Many verses in the Bible support and confirm that statement, yet a large number of Christians have failed to realize the significance of God's desire to guide and direct even the smallest details of our daily walk. While we may have no trouble believing that he has a home prepared for us in heaven, we live and act as though we are entirely on our own while we live in the flesh. In doing so, we miss out on his perfect will for our lives, as revealed so forcefully by Jeremiah 29:11:

> "For I know the plans I have for you," declares the Lord,
> "plans to prosper you and not to harm you,
> plans to give you hope and a future."

If you are unemployed, I encourage you to write out several copies of Jeremiah 29:11 and tape them up in conspicuous spots throughout your home. Every time you see one, read it out loud and claim it for your life. Memorize it, meditate on it, speak it forth throughout the day, and let it sink deeply into your spirit. Every time you do that, you remind the devil of what God's Word says about your life. It is no accident that Paul referred to God's Word as the "sword of the Spirit" (Ephesians 6:17).

Hosea 4:6 states, "my people are destroyed for lack of knowledge." If it is true that God has a plan already worked out for our lives, including the work that he wants us to do, then we should not rest until we know what that plan is. On our own, we tend to drift into occupations purely by chance, without giving a great deal of thought to the purposes of God. The good news is that our Father is anxious to provide us with valuable insight into how we can choose the right occupation.

We Are God's Workmanship

According to Bible scholars, the book of 1 Thessalonians is one of the earliest of Paul's letters to be included in the canon of Scripture. In this first letter to the Thessalonian Church, Paul gives some basic, straightforward teaching on how Christians should live as individuals and as a community of believers. It is no coincidence that Paul begins this first letter with some absolutely profound truths pertaining to God's direct involvement in our lives: "We continually remember before our God and Father your work produced by faith, your labor prompted by love, and your endurance inspired by hope in our Lord Jesus Christ" (1 Thessalonians 1:3). Writing under the guidance of the Holy Spirit, Paul states that:

a. There is a direct relationship between our faith in God and our life's work,
b. All of our endeavours are directly influenced by our love, and
c. Our ability to endure hardship will depend on our having a solid hope in Christ.

I believe Paul is saying, "Let us begin with the basics—the foundational truths on which all human enterprise was designed by God." In his letter to the church at Ephesus, Paul declares, "For we are God's workmanship, created in Christ Jesus to do good works, which God prepared in advance for us to do" (Ephesians 2:10). God not only has a plan for our life, but he has given us the blueprint for achieving his plan. Perhaps it is time that we stop to examine exactly what God had in mind when he created us.

According to Paul, God is the Master of all work. "There are different kinds of working, but the same God works all of them through all men" (1 Corinthians 12:6). It should not be surprising to us, therefore, that our faith in God will lead us into the work that he has planned for us. God created us for a specific purpose, and he wants to reveal that purpose to us. We were born with a unique set of genes. No one else in the world is exactly like us. We were given abilities, aptitudes, and interests that will equip us to carry out a specific role that God has set aside just for us.

God placed the first man, Adam, in the Garden of Eden "to work it and take care of it" (Genesis 2:15). Jesus, the second Adam, said to God, "I have brought you glory on earth by completing the work you gave me to do" (John 17:4). Jesus said to us, "I tell you the truth, anyone who has faith in me will do what I have been doing. He will do even greater things than these, because I am going to the Father. And I will do whatever you ask in my name, so that the Son may bring glory to the Father" (John 14:12–13). In Acts 13:2, we read, "While they were worshiping the Lord and fasting, the Holy Spirit said, 'Set apart for me Barnabas and Saul for the work to which I have called them.'" When we line up with God's purpose for our lives, all three members of the triune God are directly involved in our daily work.

1. God works, carrying out his plan for the world through people. The New Living Translation states 1 Corinthians 12:6 as follows: "There are different ways God works in our lives, but it is the same God who does the work through all of us." God will work through you—if you allow him.

2. Through his finished work on the cross, Jesus enables all of us to overcome the devil, the world, and our own sinful nature in order to accomplish the work that God has set before us. According to Romans 8:34, Jesus is now seated at the right hand of God *where he intercedes for us.* God has already planned our destiny, and in partnership with Jesus, we can achieve that destiny for the glory of God. "In him we were also chosen, having been predestined according to the plan of him who works out everything in conformity with the purpose of his will, in order that we, who were the first to hope in Christ, might be for the praise of his glory" (Ephesians 1:11–12 emphasis added).

3. Before departing to be with the Father, Jesus said to his disciples, "I have much more to say to you, more than you can now bear. But when He, the Spirit of truth, comes, *he will guide you into all truth.* He will not speak on his own; he will speak only what he hears, and he will tell you what is yet to come. He will bring glory to me by taking from what is mine and making it known to you" (John 16:12–14, emphasis added). Writing to the Romans, Paul said, "and he who searches our hearts knows the mind of the Spirit, because *the Spirit intercedes for the saints* in accordance with God's will" (Romans 8:27 emphasis added).

God has a job all picked out for you. You have both Jesus and the Holy Spirit interceding to the Father on your behalf, and the Holy Spirit wants to be your guidance counselor.

Work Produced by Faith

We often hear people talk about the works of God, never stopping to realize that God carries out his works through people. God uses our faith—yours and mine—to produce the work, accomplishments, or results that he desires. The Holy Spirit births faith in us when we read and listen to his Word: "so then faith cometh by hearing, and hearing by the word of God" (Romans 10:17, KJV). My faith is different from your faith, and yours is different from your neighbor's, but the source of our faith is the same God.

> "Now faith is being sure of what we hope for and certain of what we do not see" (Hebrews 11:1).

> "Do not think of yourself more highly than you ought, but rather think of yourself with sober judgment, in accordance with the measure of faith God has given you" (Romans 12:3).

> "We live by faith, not by sight" (2 Corinthians 5:7).

> "This is the victory that has overcome the world, even our faith" (1 John 5:4b).

According to the book of James, faith without works—or action—is dead. For every action by God, there should be a response by man. In the case of faith, we respond to God with our *faithfulness.*

"And without faith it is impossible to please God, because anyone who comes to him must believe that he exists and that he rewards those who earnestly seek him" (Hebrews 11:6).

Proverbs 29:18 says, "Where there is no vision, the people perish". The Hebrew word for *vision* could just as well be interpreted as "dream." Do we have a dream? Do we stop to think about or look to see where we would like to be five or ten years from now? Do we have a vision for our life? Paul says that we serve a God "who is able to do immeasurably more than all we ask or imagine, according to his power that is at work within us" (Ephesians 3:20).

Many of us travel through life having no concept of the great plans God has for us, but the Bible is filled with examples of people who were called by God out of obscurity to become great examples of faith. These heroes of the faith all have one thing in common: they all pursued and achieved exploits that would have been utterly impossible to achieve in their own strength. The call of God will always take us beyond our current level of knowledge, wisdom, or understanding so that God can be our source of strength and supply.

"Therefore, I urge you, brothers, in view of God's mercy, to offer your bodies as living sacrifices, holy and pleasing to God—this is your spiritual act of worship. Do not conform any longer to the pattern of this world, but be transformed by the renewing of your mind. Then you will be able to test and approve what God's will is—his good, pleasing and perfect will." (Romans 12:1–2). The apostle Paul tells us—in plain and simple language—how we can know God's purpose for our lives. First, we must offer—or commit—our entire lives to God, concentrate on living a holy life to please him, and focus on the task of renewing our minds.

Let Paul's own words teach us how to receive a renewed mind: "However, as it is written: 'No eye has seen, no ear has heard, no mind has conceived what God has prepared for those who love him'—but God has revealed it to us by his Spirit. The Spirit searches all things, even the deep things of God. For who among men knows the thoughts of a man except the man's spirit within him? In the same way no one knows the thoughts of God except the Spirit of God. We have not received the spirit of the world but the Spirit who is from God, that we may understand what God has freely given us. This is what we speak, not in words taught us by human wisdom but in words taught by the Spirit, expressing spiritual truths in spiritual words. The man without the Spirit does not accept the things that come from the Spirit of God, for they are foolishness to him, and he cannot understand them, because they are spiritually discerned. The spiritual man makes judgments about all things, but he himself is not subject to any man's judgment: 'For who has known the mind of the Lord that he may instruct him?' *But we have the mind of Christ"* (1 Corinthians 2:9–16, emphasis added).

Our faith in God is the key to finding his purpose and calling for our lives. Despite his old age, Abraham had faith in God's promise that he would father many nations. The Word says that his faith was considered as righteousness in the eyes of God, and the promise was fulfilled. The faith of Abraham was a simple faith, not wrapped up in high-sounding theories and doctrines. He simply believed God.

I like the way that F. F. Bosworth described faith. He was used mightily by the Lord to bring healing to many thousands in the first half of the twentieth century, and he also had a simple faith. He said, "Faith is governed by the pure Word of God, and is nothing less than expecting God to do what he promises—treating him like an honest being."

Prayerfully examine your heart, determine God's promise for your life, and then ask Jesus to deliver the faith you need to see the fruit of that promise.

Labor Prompted by Love

The apostle Paul makes a very profound statement in Galatians 5:6b. According to Paul, "The only thing that counts is faith, expressing itself in love." He was speaking to the religious legalists of his day, who insisted on forcing every believer to follow their traditions of the law. But Paul rebuked them, saying, "the entire law is summed up in a single command: 'Love your neighbor as yourself.'" James calls that the "royal law" (James 2:8), and in Romans 13:10, Paul writes "Love does no harm to its neighbor. Therefore love is the fulfillment of the law."

Perhaps the very best expression of God's love is found in 1 Corinthians 13, where Paul explains in detail just what love is—and what it is not. If you are not familiar with it, stop now and read it. Paul concludes the chapter by declaring, "and now these three remain: faith, hope, and love. But the greatest of these is love." The writings of John—both his Gospel and Epistles—are filled with descriptions and examples of the love of God as taught and demonstrated by Jesus. One of the most profound truths in the Bible is found in 1 John 4:19: "We love because he first loved us."

"This is how we know what love is: Jesus Christ laid down his life for us. And we ought to lay down our lives for our brothers. If anyone has material possessions and sees his brother in need but has no pity on him, how can the love of God be in him? Dear children, let us not love with words or tongue but with actions and in truth" (1 John 3:16–18). "By this all men will know that you are my disciples, if you love one another" (John 13:35).

These verses—and many like them—point directly to one of the best-kept secrets in the world. It is a powerful and unfailing principle of God's kingdom that success and favor will come to those who know how to serve others in Christian love. The others I am referring to include our bosses, our fellow employees, and those who may work under us. It includes

Christians and non-Christians. Every occupation, job, or position in the world is a mission field for the Lord Jesus. If we truly serve others in kindness and in the love of God, we will receive favor from God and other people—but there is a cost.

Jesus once told his disciples, "If anyone would come after me, he must deny himself and take up his cross daily and follow me. For whoever wants to save his life will lose it, but whoever loses his life for me will save it" (Luke 9:23–24). In effect, Jesus said that if we are willing to stop thinking of only ourselves and start putting the needs of others ahead of our own needs just as he did, then our life would be *sozo,* which in the Greek language can be interpreted to mean any of the following: "delivered, protected, healed, preserved, saved, or made whole." Genuine satisfaction in life is found through serving other people in the name and spirit of Jesus.

We live in a troubled world, and God wants to use us as a channel for the love and compassion of Christ to touch the lives of those around us with his brand of comfort. When trouble or difficulties arise, we Christians are inclined to ask ourselves: "Why would a loving God allow this to happen, especially when I am trying hard to serve him?" Paul answers this question in his second letter to the Church at Corinth: "Praise be to the God and Father of our Lord Jesus Christ, the Father of compassion and the God of all comfort, who comforts us in all our troubles, so that we can comfort those in any trouble with the comfort we ourselves have received from God. For just as the sufferings of Christ flow over into our lives, so also through Christ our comfort overflows" (2 Corinthians 1:3–5). The truth is that we cannot give away something that we have not already received.

Matthew said of Jesus: "When he saw the crowds, he had compassion on them, because they were harassed and helpless, like sheep without a shepherd" (Matthew 9:36). If there is one lesson that this generation must learn, it is this:

Our love is only possible because of Christ's love, which he has already placed in our hearts by the Holy Spirit, and that same love must be the driving force of our lives. "For Christ's love compels us, because we are convinced that one died for all, and therefore all died. And he died for all, that those who live should no longer live for themselves but for him who died for them and was raised again" (2 Corinthians 5:14–15). If the love of Christ is truly in us, we will find the courage and the strength to set aside our selfish activities in order that others may see and experience the compassionate love of Christ Jesus through us.

How can we serve others in love in our workplace? As an employee, your first job while at work is to do all in your power to make your boss successful and to be helpful and cooperative with all those you work with. Do this in the love of Christ, and pray continuously for those with whom you work. If you work in a business that provides products or services to others, God's royal law of love requires that you adopt the role of servant toward your customers and suppliers at all times.

According to 1 Corinthians 13, all of the faith and hope in the world will be largely ineffective unless applied with a heaping dose of love. In the vast majority of cases, love is manifested not in words of endearment, but in a spirit of service to those around us. If you help a fellow worker solve a problem or learn a new skill, or if you patiently listen to and encourage someone in the lunch room who is going through deep waters of hurt and despair, you are demonstrating to them the love of Christ.

About now, some readers are thinking, *Oh, but you don't know my last employer* or *you haven't met that person who worked right beside me!* Most of us know very few people who would qualify as legitimate enemies, but we know at least a few whom we would like to see chosen as first emigrants to the moon. Of all the people we know, these are the people who need Jesus most. If we don't show them the love of Jesus, who will? It is just possible that God may have placed us near them for a purpose. Our labors that are truly prompted by love will always be honored and blessed by our heavenly Father.

Endurance Inspired by Hope

The first chapter touched briefly on the purpose of hope in our lives as it relates to our eternal home in heaven, but the ministry of God's hope in our lives goes much further and deeper than that. Hope is much more than wishful thinking. Just as the Holy Spirit gives the hope of eternal life to us as new believers, the same Spirit continues throughout our lives to broaden and deepen that hope. The Holy Spirit never points to himself, but instead points to Jesus. Just as trust is the outworking of faith in our lives and serving others is the outworking of love, the manifestation of hope in our life is our ever-increasing confidence in the blood of Jesus to give us power over sin, the flesh, and the devil. The job description of the Holy Spirit is to manifest (or reveal) the life and ministry of Jesus through his believers (1 Corinthians 12:8). Because of the Holy Spirit, Jesus could state that all those who would place their faith in him could do "even greater things" than he himself had done on earth! (John 14:12). Because Paul had seen the power of God working through his life by the Holy Spirit, he could confidently state that this Spirit within you is the same Spirit that raised Jesus from the dead (Romans 8:11). When believers grasp the full truth of these statements and many more like them in the New Testament, their whole lives will be transformed. There will be new levels of confidence, boldness, and strength to endure as they begin to identify with the sufferings of Christ: "but we also rejoice in our sufferings, because we know that suffering produces perseverance; perseverance, character; and character, hope. And hope does not disappoint us" (Romans 5:3–5).

This is a pivotal verse of scripture for those who would like to understand the meaning of hope. Paul is saying that:

- Difficult situations teach us to have perseverance as we deal with life's problems.
- Patiently and consistently dealing with problems will produce in us a testimony of being worthy of trust, defined by the world as *character.*
- Trustworthiness and character will birth in us new levels of confidence and boldness as we step out in the "hope of sharing in the harvest" (1 Corinthians 9:10).

Jesus' last words from the cross were, "It is finished" (John 19:30). Three days later, God would raise him from the dead. All of his disciples (except Judas) and many of his close friends would see him. According to 1 Corinthians 15:6, more than 500 people would testify that they had seen him physically walking the streets of Jerusalem. Then he would be taken up to Heaven before the eyes of his disciples (Acts 1:9).

Because Jesus died in our place, we can have absolute confidence that he has the power and authority to forgive us and cleanse us from all of our sins. Because Jesus took the punishment that we deserve, we can rest in the assurance that he can bring peace and healing into the lives of all who call on his Name. Because of his resurrection, we can experience his power working in our lives to help us overcome every habit, bondage, and worry. We can have intimate fellowship with God and Jesus through the living presence of his Holy Spirit in our hearts. This is the hope that will carry us through any situation or difficulty that the world or the devil would throw at us, including unemployment.

Not many of us will be asked to enter a lion's den (Daniel 6:16), but when we declare our hope in Christ to unsaved relatives and fellow workers, we may often feel like we are in there with Daniel. There is a growing cynicism toward Christianity among unbelievers today, and it often takes perseverance that only the Holy Spirit can provide to represent the risen Christ to them.

Not many of us will be required to enter a fiery furnace as the Hebrew children did in the third chapter of Daniel, but we will all be tested by the refiner's fire when we must take a stand against evil, which is rapidly taking over our streets, schools, and mass media. It is going to take people of real, honest-to-goodness character to walk through the insults that the world will hurl at us when we refuse to follow the crowd and when we choose ways of holiness and righteousness.

It is interesting to note that the root word used for *hope* in the Hebrew language is interpreted as "cord." The same Hebrew word is used to describe the scarlet cord used by Rahab to save her entire family in Joshua 2:18. According to the dictionary, a cord is a "string or small rope of twisted strands or fibers." Throughout our Christian walk, God will place us in situations that will test our faith (James 1:3). As we search the scriptures to find answers to life's problems, we begin personalizing the promises of God, which God then spins into a strand of ever-increasing faith. And as we accept our responsibility to bring the light of Jesus into each difficult situation, God produces in us a string of testimony called character. Then, as faith and character combine to form the strong cord of hope, we can begin to grasp "how wide and long and high and deep is the love of Christ" (Ephesians 3:16–19).

"We have this hope as an anchor for the soul, firm and secure. *It enters the inner sanctuary behind the curtain* where Jesus, who went before us, has entered on our behalf. He has become a high priest forever, in the order of Melchizedek" (Hebrews 6:19–20, emphasis added). Through the death and resurrection of Christ Jesus, the Bible tells us that our hope can transport us beyond the veil into the Holy of Holies to become a "royal priesthood" (1 Peter 2:9), with Jesus as our high priest. My finite mind has great difficulty in comprehending that!

Faith, love, and hope—these are three small but powerful words that will have profound influence on our ability to lead a happy and fulfilling life. We cannot buy them from any store or catalogue, but they are free to all who are willing to pay the price of following Jesus. No degree of education—either secular or Christian—can guarantee that we will walk in them.

Genuine faith, genuine love, and genuine hope are affairs of the heart (Hebrews 10:22, 1 Peter 1:22, Ephesians 1:18). Any faith, love, or hope that exists only in our minds or emotions is counterfeit and will eventually lead to disappointment. Like Paul, I pray that we might receive from God the Spirit of wisdom and revelation so that we might achieve the work that he planned for us from the beginning of time.

Life Application—Chapter 4

A. The question is often asked: "How will I know when I have truly heard from God?" I believe that there are at least four significant tests that one can apply. Look up the scriptures below and summarize the ways that we can know when we are moving in the will of the Father.

Desires of the Heart—Psalm 37:4; Psalm 145:18–19

The Umpire of Peace—2 Corinthians 2:12–13; Psalm 85:8; Psalm 119:165; Isaiah 26:3

The Second Witness—Deuteronomy 19:15; Acts 11:12; Acts 15:28; Romans 8:16

Freedom (Release) of the Spirit—John 16:13–14; John 8:31–32; Galatians 5:1, 13

B. The Bible mentions some 218 different occupations, only twelve of which would be considered spiritual or religious in nature. The remaining 206 occupations would be called secular in today's terms. Oddly enough, when God chose who would lead his people in times of major crisis or change, he often looked to the laypersons instead of the religious leaders of the day. Almost without exception, the great heroes of the Old Testament were working in non-religious occupations when God called them. When Jesus (who was trained as a carpenter) began his ministry on earth, he called twelve disciples to be his first students, all of whom came from secular jobs. This does not in any way reflect negatively on those who carry the title of pastor, priest, or rabbi, but it does illustrate that "God is no respecter of persons" (Acts 10:34, KJV). Here are just four examples:

1 Samuel 16:7; 1 Samuel 16:10–13

Amos 1:1; Amos 7:14–15

Mark 1:16–17

Acts 4:13

Chapter 5—EXAMINE YOURSELF

The preparation of a resume is an integral part of most re-employment programs and services. In order to complete a resume, it is necessary for a person to spend time recording vital qualifications such as education, training, and experience in the workplace. If you are unemployed and you have not yet prepared a resume to assist in your job search, you should develop one.

While you are taking stock, it would also be a good idea to do a spiritual inventory. In his second letter to the church at Corinth, Paul wrote, "Examine yourselves to see whether you are in the faith; test yourselves. Do you not realize that Christ Jesus is in you—unless, of course, you fail the test" (2 Corinthians 13:5). *We can't expect God to help us achieve our employment goals if we are not living our lives in ways that are pleasing to him.* A spiritual inventory allows us to take stock of our lives from God's perspective.

A secondary, but equally important benefit of this exercise will be what the apostle Paul called a *transformed mind.* Romans 12:2 reads "Do not conform any longer to the pattern of this world, but be transformed by the renewing of your mind. Then you will be able to test and approve what God's will is — his good, pleasing and perfect will." Remember all of those negative thoughts and emotions listed in the early pages of this study? When you understand and appropriate for yourself the personality and attributes that God wants to give you, you will have no need of psychology books, because the Bible says emphatically that we can have the "mind of Christ" (1 Corinthians 2:16).

In his sermon on the mount, Jesus literally turned traditional values upside-down. Beginning with the Beatitudes, Jesus declared a brand-new standard of behavior for those who wish to serve God. Jesus repeatedly used the phrase, "You have heard it said … but I tell you," and the Bible says that the crowd went away "amazed at his teaching" (Matthew 7:28). For instance, Jesus taught people to love their enemies, and to do good to those who oppose them. But we find it natural to hate our enemies, not to love them. We prefer to take an eye for an eye instead of turning the other cheek. We seek to store up treasures here on earth rather than in heaven as he taught. To the human mind, the Sermon on the Mount calls for a radical change in the way we think. Contrary to popular opinion, the principles put forward by Jesus are not a spiritual straightjacket, but they are literal keys to freedom. They provide a virtual road map for those who seriously desire to recover order, peace, and health in their lives.

And so the question that begs an answer is, "What qualities, temperaments, or mindset will allow us to live successfully in this upside-down world that Jesus teaches?" If we are to do an honest evaluation of ourselves—and if we truly want to see ourselves as God sees us—we will need a standard, a benchmark, or a kind of universal spiritual job description in order to carry out any kind of measurement. It might be tempting to compare our lives to one of the major characters mentioned in the Bible, but that could be misleading, because each one of us has been given unique talents and purpose for our lives. We cannot live someone else's life. If we attempt to compare ourselves to Jesus, we will run the danger of becoming overwhelmed by the absolute perfection and holiness of his life—to the point where we might give up.

We need a standard that applies to everyone—but one which is clear, concise, and realistic. I looked for such a standard of measurement in God's Word for several years, and the one that I found was a complete surprise. Consistent with the rest of Jesus' teaching, it is one that will appear to be totally upside-down to the natural mind. It is found in the first three verses of Matthew 18, where Jesus' disciples came to him with the question, "Who is the greatest in the kingdom of heaven?"

According to Mark's gospel, this conversation took place in Capernaum, a small fishing village on the northern shore of the Sea of Galilee, which served as a home base for much of Jesus' public ministry over its three years. On a recent trip to Israel, I stood beneath a sycamore tree at the site of the synagogue where Jesus taught in Capernaum. In my mind's eye, I could imagine the whole scenario of Matthew's account. Jesus may have been resting with his back against a tree similar to the one that was providing me with shade. His disciples were probably seated before him, perhaps in a loose circle. It could have taken place in front of the apostle Peter's small home, which has been excavated and positively identified, almost next door to the synagogue.

Jesus had no doubt been watching some children playing along the narrow dirt road. We know from Mark 10:14 that Jesus was a close friend of the children wherever he went. Now he called a little child, and had the child stand among the disciples. I could picture the child, dusty and dirty from a hard day's play, looking up into the face of Jesus—loving him, and hoping to hear another of his wonderful stories about God. But Jesus turned to his disciples and began to teach.

"I tell you the truth, unless you change and become like little children, you will never enter the kingdom of heaven. Therefore, whoever humbles himself like this child is the greatest in the kingdom of heaven" (Matthew 18:3–4). Did you hear what Jesus said? Is it possible that some people may miss his kingdom altogether, if they fail to become humble like a child? I believe Jesus meant exactly what he said. In Mark 10:14–15, Jesus is quoted as saying, "Let the little children come to me, and do not hinder them, for the kingdom of God belongs to such as these. I tell you the truth, anyone who will not receive the kingdom of God like a little child will never enter it." For that reason, we need to examine the character traits that distinguish a little child from an adult and check to see if we pass the test. How do we stack up against the greatest in the kingdom of heaven? Here are seven basic characteristics of a child that will provide focus for our self-examination.

Before being contaminated by the world, most young children are by nature:

> humble
> honest
> forgiving
> tenderhearted
> obedient
> meek
> peacemakers

If you need a scriptural reference for the validity of these characteristics, refer to Proverbs 6:16–19 for a list of the exact opposite traits, which are identified as those things which God hates in a person:

> There are six things the Lord hates, seven that are detestable to him:
> haughty eyes,
> a lying tongue,
> hands that shed innocent blood,
> a heart that devises wicked schemes,

feet that are quick to rush into evil,
a false witness who pours out lies and
a man who stirs up dissension among brothers.

The remainder of this chapter will guide you through each of these seven characteristics in order to respond to Paul's admonition to examine yourself.

Get some paper and a pencil and find a comfortable place to be alone with your thoughts for a while. Begin by praying for God's wisdom and insight. Ask God to help you discern those truths that he would have you know. Write your responses to each question in point form after first giving serious consideration to your life in the light of each child-like quality. The results are for your own personal use and don't need to be shared with others unless you choose to do so. Your goal is to identify those areas of your life where you need God's help in order to become more like the "greatest in the kingdom of heaven."

This is not a test that you can pass or fail. It is simply a means of seeing for yourself the degree of your "growing in the knowledge of God" (Colossians 1:10). Every area of your life—including your work and your career—will be positively affected by bringing your life in line with God's definition of a true Christian.

A. Humble

According to Proverbs 6:16–18, God hates haughty eyes—so much so that he places this as the very first item on his list of abominations. *Haughty* means "proud, arrogant, vain, scornful or self-satisfied." The Hebrew word used here carries the connotation of being walled in, unconcerned about anyone else.

Jesus began the greatest sermon ever preached with the words, "Blessed are the poor in spirit, for theirs is the kingdom of heaven" (Matthew 5:3). To his disciples, Jesus declared, "whoever humbles himself like this little child is the greatest in the kingdom of heaven" (Matthew 18:4). Obviously, the very first key to living the life that God intends for us is the key of humility. Like children, we need to have a right estimate of ourselves. Children are not prone to pride or arrogance. They know very well that they have much to learn, and they are not the least bit embarrassed to admit that they need help.

If you have any doubts about the foundational importance of humility in preparing us to walk with God, read what the Lord said to Solomon one night: "If my people, who are called by my name, will humble themselves and pray and seek my face and turn from their wicked ways, then I will hear from heaven and will forgive their sin and will heal their land" (2 Chronicles 7:14). It is our humility that first opens the door to seeking God, then to repentance and right living—which in turn will bring God's forgiveness and restoration. That pattern is consistent from Genesis to Revelation.

Humility is a heart attitude, one that enables us to admit that we don't have all the answers. Humility has nothing to do with humiliation, self-abasement, or low self-esteem. A humble person is modest, lowly, and unpretentious. Humility cannot exist where there is a proud spirit, and pride cannot exist where there is a humble spirit.

Many times we may try to take on a humble approach to life—but before long, we have slipped back into a self-centred attitude. We need to understand that there is a second part to the process of becoming humble. Peter speaks about this in his second epistle: "Humble yourselves, therefore, under God's mighty hand, that he may lift you up in due time. Cast all your anxiety [cares (KJV)] on him because he cares for you" (1 Peter 5:6–7). If we hope to be successful in remaining humble, it is vital that we learn to give over all of our worries, problems, and fears to God, and leave them there. Otherwise, the process of worrying and struggling to solve our problems in our own strength will cause us to step back onto the throne of our lives. A preacher once testified that he was, at one time in his life, almost overwhelmed by his financial burdens and responsibilities. In obedience to 1 Peter 5:7, he began placing his monthly bills in a stack, holding them over his head, and simply saying, "Lord, here are your bills for the month—you look after them." That simple act gave him the peace he needed in order to get on with his ministry, trusting God to meet his needs. That testimony helped me overcome a life-long habit of worrying.

Notice that we must humble *ourselves.* God will not do it for us, because he gave us freedom of choice. The most he will do is to place us in situations or circumstances that will lead to humility. "Remember how the Lord your God led you all the way in the desert these forty years, to humble you and to test you in order to know what was in your heart, whether or not you would keep his commands" (Deuteronomy 8:2). If periods of unemployment can do anything, they certainly help us relate to the desert experience of the Hebrew children.

Unemployment is like a desert. We can wander around in our pride, rebellion, and self-pity—or we can choose to acknowledge God (through Jesus) as our source of supply and blessing. In many ways, a period of unemployment represents a crossroads in our life. We can choose to do things our way or God's way. Jesus pointed to the best direction: "Take my yoke upon you and learn from me, for I am gentle and humble in heart, and you will find rest for your souls" (Matthew 11:29). "Your attitude should be the same as that of Christ Jesus: Who, being in very nature God, did not consider equality with God something to be grasped, but made himself nothing, taking the very nature of a servant, being made in human likeness. And being found in appearance as a man, he humbled himself and became obedient to death—even death on a cross!" (Philippians 2:5–8).

If Jesus, who was the Son of the living God, humbled himself in order to please God, how much more do you and I need to follow that example? In Matthew 23:12, Jesus says, "For whoever exalts himself will be humbled, and whoever humbles himself will be exalted." In Acts 17:6, Paul and Silas were accused by the religious leaders of the day to be "these that have turned the world upside down" (KJV). To an ordinary human, God's ways do seem to be upside-down. Jesus taught that it is our ways—not God's—which are really upside-down. "'For my thoughts are not your thoughts, neither are your ways my ways,' declares the Lord" (Isaiah 55:8). If you want tangible evidence of this, study the words of Jesus in the Sermon on the Mount beginning in Matthew 5, and record the number of times Jesus called for a radically new way of thinking. People who learn to think God's way will discover that his way is much better.

A large number of studies have been published over recent years on subjects like team-building and employee empowerment, and these have had a dramatic impact in the labor market. Most employers today are searching for people who are prepared to work in close cooperation with others. They seek people who know how to communicate effectively with fellow workers in team problem-solving situations. There is not much demand for lone rangers in today's labor market. Larger employers frequently use a series of tests and interviews to ensure that new employees will succeed in a team setting. Workers have changed, too. Most workers today want to have some input into how they do their work, and they may not remain in a job that turns them into a robot.

As a result of these changes, many employers are now looking for workers who demonstrate good people skills—even for jobs that have little or no public contact. A person who has learned to walk in humility and is willing to listen to and seriously consider the thoughts and suggestions of fellow workers at any level of the organization will have a definite edge in most job interviews. Once employed, the person who demonstrates Christ-like humility will continuously seek to follow Paul's advice to "Be devoted to one another in brotherly love. Honor one another above yourselves" (Romans 12:10).

If you have been—or have aspired to be—in a position of supervision or management of other workers, it is doubly important that you learn to walk in humility. If you study biographies of the world's great leaders, you will discover that almost without exception, they were humble people. It was the spirit of humility that allowed them to win the support and confidence of employees and associates. Humble people don't build walls, but they teach others by their example how to tear down walls and be successful in their own right. If you want to be seen as a successful manager, you must first learn how to develop successful employees. Successful employees will make you a successful manager.

A humble spirit is absolutely essential for those who would please God.

Am I humble?

Life Application—Am I Humble?

Let these verses help you in your self-evaluation:

Isaiah 66:2b

Philippians 2:3

James 3:13

1 Peter 5:5

B. Honest

The book of Proverbs says that God hates a lying tongue (Proverbs 6:17). Due to their innocent nature, young children are sometimes painfully honest. If you happen to be bald or overweight, you know exactly what I am talking about. As children gain understanding, most children learn that some things—however true—are better left unsaid. James wrote, "everyone should be quick to listen, slow to speak" (James 1:19).

The Bible says that *all* liars will be turned away from entering heaven (Revelation 21:8). Jesus had a way of looking beyond our actions and showing us that most of our problems begin with our hearts. He said, "out of the overflow of the heart the mouth speaks" (Matthew 12:34). Paul wrote, "You were taught, with regard to your former way of life, to put off your old self, which is being corrupted by its deceitful desires; to be made new in the attitude of your minds; and to put on the new self, created to be like God in true righteousness and holiness. Therefore each of you must put off falsehood and speak truthfully to his neighbor, for we are all members of one body" (Ephesians 4:22–25). Lying begins with a deceitful heart and attitude. One of the first real evidences of the new birth in Christ is our willingness to admit that we have sinned, we have no one to blame but ourselves, and that Jesus has forgiven us of all unrighteousness.

Another sign that a person is really born again is their newly found hunger for the Word of God—particularly the teachings of Jesus. At that point in their walk, people need to hear the promise of Jesus found in John 16:13: "But when He, the Spirit of truth, comes, he will guide you into all truth." Left to their own devices, people will have a natural tendency to look to the teachings and writings of others to find truth. In their search for meaning in life, people often turn to other religions and philosophies. To Christians of his day, the apostle Paul wrote, "See to it that no one takes you captive through hollow and deceptive philosophy, which depends on human tradition and the basic principles of this world rather than on Christ" (Colossians 2:8). Your Bible is the ultimate guide to all truth. Any teaching or philosophy that does not line up with the Word of God will eventually lead to deception. Those who are deceived become deceivers, and the cancer spreads.

Unfortunately, Christians who attempt to obey the Scriptures and "speak the truth in love" (Ephesians 4:15) frequently encounter rebuke from a world that does not want to hear the truth. That is why Jesus said, "Blessed are those who are persecuted because of righteousness, for theirs is the kingdom of heaven. Blessed are you when people insult you, persecute you and falsely say all kinds of evil against you because of me. Rejoice and be glad, because great is your reward in heaven, for in the same way they persecuted the prophets who were before you" (Matthew 5:10–12). During his three years of ministry, Jesus was constantly questioned, ridiculed, and eventually persecuted in extreme fashion by the religious rulers of his day because he dared to ask them to repent of their sins—and he had the audacity to truthfully declare that he was the Christ. Jesus never backed away from truth, even when it meant he would be crucified. And Jesus told us who followed that we would also have a cross of persecution to bear if we truly follow him (Luke 14:27).

Persecution of Christians is a fact in many parts of the world today. Conversion to the Christian faith in some cultures can lead to instant rejection by family and friends. In a few countries, it is a crime punishable by death to attempt to lead others to Christ. In Western culture, the persecution of Christians is subtler. You may have already encountered a neighbor who laughs at your "fundamentalist" beliefs and calls them nonsense, a political enthusiast who insists that Christianity has no place in government or in public meetings, or a social activist who believes that demonstrations and picket lines are more important than going to church. All of these are examples of a society that has failed to recognize the truth of the Bible. If you dare to oppose them, they will almost always attack your Christian beliefs, calling them outdated, exclusivist, and irrelevant to the problems of today.

"This is the verdict: Light has come into the world, but men loved darkness instead of light because their deeds were evil" (John 3:19). To the person who is living without God's light, the concepts of light and truth can be very fearful. Paul stated it well: "But thanks be to God, who always leads us in triumphal procession in Christ and through us spreads everywhere the fragrance of the knowledge of him. For we are to God the aroma of Christ among those who are being saved and those who are perishing. To the one we are the smell of death; to the other, the fragrance of life" (2 Corinthians 2:14–16). When you begin to understand this, you can learn to endure criticism and even persecution with the mind of Christ, who once said, "Father, forgive them, for they do not know what they are doing" (Luke 23:34).

Jesus would say to us, "you are the light of the world. A city on a hill cannot be hidden. Neither do people light a lamp and put it under a bowl. Instead they put it on its stand, and it gives light to everyone in the house. In the same way, let your light shine before men, that they may see your good deeds and praise your Father in heaven" (Matthew 5:14–16). The light of God is his Word, and his Word is truth.

Some of the people reading these words have lost their jobs because of their own actions. The reasons are many and varied, but our initial human reaction to job dismissal can sometimes take on a form of denial, blame-shifting, or self-justification. Jesus teaches us that it is all right to admit that we blew it, if that is true. This is a time when we desperately need to be honest with God, other people, and—most importantly—with ourselves.

Other people who have recently become unemployed are struggling with feelings of guilt, shame, or even depression. After many sleepless nights and restless days, despite their seeking advice and counseling, they still cannot shake the overpowering feelings of worry and nagging thoughts of self-doubt. We need to recognize where these feelings and thoughts originate. The Bible teaches us that we have an enemy of our soul, the "accuser of our brothers, who accuses them before our God day and night" (Revelation 12:10, KJV). Jesus called this enemy a thief who "comes only to steal and kill and destroy." Then Jesus adds, "I have come that they may have life, and have it to the full" (John 10:10).

The enemy of our souls would have us dwell continuously on our shortcomings and failures. If he can, he will manipulate our thinking to the point that we believe his lies, causing an overpowering feeling of low self-esteem. Jesus would remind you, however, that you have become a child of the King, an overcomer, and precious in God's sight. The Bible says, "Resist the devil and he will flee from you" (James 4:7).

Jesus said: "I am the Way, the Truth and the Life." (John 14:6). I recently learned that the Hebrew children used those same words in reference to the three doors of the tabernacle of Moses. The door into the outer court was called the way. The door of the inner court was referred to as the truth. And the entrance to the Holy of Holies was the life. When Jesus called himself the way, the truth, and the life, he was saying that he represents the entrance to every experience and every facet of God that we will ever need. When Jesus enters a human heart, that heart becomes a tabernacle where God and people can be reconciled and have fellowship. A humble heart will guide us into the outer courts of God, because that is his way. But it will take the sacrifice of truth to get us into the inner court where the anointing oil resides.

Am I honest?

Life Application—Am I Honest?

Let these verses help you in your self-evaluation:

1 Chronicles 29:17

Zechariah 8:16

John 3:21

John 7:18

Colossians 3:9–10

C. Forgiving

How many times has this scene presented itself? Two children are playing in a sand pile. One child begins to scream and cry; two parents come running. "She threw sand at me," one says; the other answers, "Because he hit me." The two parents enter into a lengthy and heated discussion over whose fault it is, what punishment is needed, etc. In the meantime—completely unnoticed by the parents—the two children resume playing as if nothing had happened. Children forgive and forget quickly, but adults frequently find it difficult to forgive—and harder to forget even the smallest of offences.

The book of Proverbs says that God hates hands that shed innocent blood (Proverbs 6:17), but Jesus said, "Blessed are the merciful, for they shall be shown mercy" (Matthew 5:7). I don't expect that many people reading these words will have blood on their hands, but listen to what Jesus said in the middle of his Sermon on the Mount: "You have heard that it was said to the people long ago, 'Do not murder, and anyone who murders will be subject to judgment.' But I tell you that anyone who is angry with his brother will be subject to judgment" (Matthew 5:21–22a). Being angry with your neighbor is equivalent to murdering him or her in the spirit. How many of us as children learned to say to our adversaries, "sticks and stones may break my bones, but names will never hurt me"? We knew as we said it that it was not true, because those names, the taunts, and the put-downs really hurt right down where we live. How many of us have been caught up in situations of sharp disagreement with family members or neighbors where unkind words were exchanged? Sometimes it took days to get over the feeling of hurt and rejection. Some of us may still be hurting after all these months or years. We feel like something deep down inside of us died a little bit, and we cannot forget the pain. Jesus came to show us a better way and to empower us to be merciful in every situation. People who are merciful tend to be kind and forgiving, even when people try to hurt them.

When we first meet the apostle Paul in the Bible, he is a hard-nosed Pharisee named Saul who has come to be a witness to the stoning of Stephen (Acts 8:1). In Acts 9:1, we see that Saul was "breathing out murderous threats against the Lord's disciples," having permission to go to Damascus to arrest and persecute the followers of Jesus. Then something happened—he met Jesus; and his life would never be the same. Later on in life, Paul wrote, "If it is possible, as far as it depends on you, live at peace with everyone. Do not take revenge, my friends, but leave room for God's wrath, for it is written: 'It is mine to avenge; I will repay,' says the Lord. On the contrary: If your enemy is hungry, feed him; if he is thirsty, give him something to drink. In doing this, you will heap burning coals on his head. Do not be overcome by evil, but overcome evil with good" (Romans 12:18–21).

Jesus said, "Be merciful, just as your Father is merciful. Do not judge, and you will not be judged. Do not condemn, and you will not be condemned. Forgive, and you will be forgiven." (Luke 6:36–37). On another occasion, he said, "For if you forgive men when they sin against you, your heavenly Father will also forgive you. But if you do not forgive men their sins, your Father will not forgive your sin" (Matthew 6:14–15).

It is an established fact that feelings of resentment and an unwillingness to forgive can—if allowed to dominate one's thinking over a period of time—lead to serious mental or physical illness. It is as if God created us to be just like the little child who can walk away from disagreement and pick up life where he or she left off. This should be a lesson to those who lose their jobs. Don't be angry, but forgive those who caused you to be unemployed. Just like Jesus, we need to be able to pray at all times, "Father forgive them, for they do not know what they are doing" (Luke 23:34).

Am I forgiving?

Life Application—Am I Forgiving?

Let these verses help you in your self-evaluation:

Matthew 6:14–15

Matthew 18:21–35

Luke 6:31–37

2 Corinthians 2:5–11

Colossians 3:13

D. Tenderhearted

God hates a heart that devises wicked schemes (or imaginations, as the King James Version puts it) (Proverbs 6:18), but Jesus said, "Blessed are the pure in heart, for they shall see God" (Matthew 5:8). The Greek word interpreted as pure can just as well be interpreted as "clean." David asked God to renew in him a clean heart (Psalm 51:10, KJV). The Bible often refers to a wicked heart as being a hard heart. One of the first signs of true conversion in a born-again Christian is a radical change of heart. "I will give you a new heart and put a new spirit in you; I will remove from you your heart of stone and give you a heart of flesh. And I will put my Spirit in you and move you to follow my decrees and be careful to keep my laws" (Ezekiel 36:26–27). The heart of flesh is a tender heart. The word tender implies youth, vulnerability, something that is easily hurt, sensitivity, and a sympathetic nature. "And be ye kind one to another, *tenderhearted,* forgiving one another, even as God for Christ's sake hath forgiven you" (Ephesians 4:32, KJV, emphasis added).

I have never met a small child who didn't cry easily when frightened or treated badly. As they grow up, children are often programmed to be less vulnerable, not so easily hurt, and less sensitive. Well-meaning parents instinctively teach their children how to move from a situation of dependency to one of independence by encouraging attitudes of self-confidence. That is good, but we all know that too much of a good thing becomes harmful. Carried to its natural extreme, the process of becoming independent can lead to an attitude of pride and superiority.

When our youngest son was about three years old, we took the family camping. After picking out a campsite and setting up the tent trailer, Dad and the boys took the station wagon to get a load of firewood, and as soon as it began to get dark, a campfire was lit. This was a first for our three-year-old, and he sat looking at the fire, obviously in deep thought. Finally, he asked the question that was on his mind: "Do you think that God minds if we burn up his wood?" As we explained the concept of God's love to our son, I found myself wishing that I could be that sensitive about God's feelings.

The more I think about the concept of "tough love," which is popular in Christian circles today, the more I feel a need to be careful how we speak of that concept. Jesus' love was not tough, but tender, compassionate, and unconditional. The only people with whom Jesus got tough were those religious leaders and temple workers who purposely gave the appearance of loving people, but whose actions demonstrated that they loved only themselves. His words to them could hardly be called loving.

We are exhorted to "speak the truth in love" (Ephesians 4:15), and at times, the truth may not be what people want to hear. In extreme cases of disobedience or intentional disregard for God's Word, it may be necessary to "hand them over to Satan" as mentioned in 1 Corinthians 5:5 and 1 Timothy 1:20. Using Paul's model, we would do this by simply breaking fellowship with them. But to those who are struggling with life's problems and acting in ignorance of God's light, our words must always be gentle. Our instinct is to say to the sinner, "You are only getting what you deserve because of your evil deeds," but Jesus said to the woman caught in adultery, "Then neither do I condemn you ... go now and leave your life of sin" (John 8:11). There is a vast difference.

Isaiah prophesied of the coming Saviour, "A bruised reed he will not break, and a smoldering wick he will not snuff out. In faithfulness he will bring forth justice" (Isaiah 42:3).

"Above all else, guard your heart, for it is the wellspring of life" (Proverbs 4:23).

Everything you do and say will be profoundly influenced by the condition of your heart.

Is it tender?

Life Application—Am I Tenderhearted?

Let these verses help you in your self-evaluation:

Psalm 126:5–6

Daniel 4:27

Matthew 9:36

Colossians 3:12

Ephesians 4:32

1 Peter 1:22; 1 Peter 3:8

E. Obedient

According to Proverbs, God hates feet that are quick to run to evil (Proverbs 6:18), but Jesus said, "Blessed are those who hunger and thirst for righteousness, for they will be filled" (Matthew 5:6). Before being spoiled by the world, the greatest wish of any child is to please his or her parents. Children will literally jump through hoops to get their parents' attention. Watch a group of them playing in the shallow water at the beach. Their conversation is a litany of, "Watch me, mommy!" and "Look at me, daddy!" What they really want is affirmation, and at a very tender age, children instinctively know that there is a direct link between performance and acceptance, obedience and affirmation. They want to be good so their parents will love them.

Adults don't always have the same attitude toward the heavenly Father. The Bible teaches that ever since the fall of Adam, our nature has had a built-in tendency to pursue evil. When we meet Jesus and accept him into our lives, our spirit is immediately and permanently redeemed. That word *redeemed* conveys the image of being ransomed, rescued, or released from slavery. Unfortunately, our physical bodies were not redeemed at the same time (Romans 8:10). We still continue to grow older, and in a sense, we die a little bit each day in our bodies. Worse than that, the old sin nature is still alive and well in our bodies. Our physical nature has the same hungers and drives that it had before God redeemed our spirit. And so we experience a battle between our spirit—which seeks to serve God—and our flesh—which wishes to please only itself.

Listen to the words of Paul found in his letter to the Romans: "So I find this law at work: When I want to do good, evil is right there with me. For in my inner being I delight in God's law; but I see another law at work in the members of my body, waging war against the law of my mind and making me a prisoner of the law of sin at work within my members. What a wretched man I am! Who will rescue me from this body of death?" (Romans 7:21–24). Later on in the same letter, Paul gives us the answer to that question: "Do not conform any longer to the pattern of this world, but be transformed by the renewing of your mind. Then you will be able to test and approve what God's will is—his good, pleasing and perfect will" (Romans 12:2).

Paul recognized that spiritual warfare was going on in his mind. He spoke more about this warfare in his second letter to the church at Corinth, where he concluded, "The weapons we fight with are not the weapons of the world. On the contrary, they have divine power to demolish strongholds. We demolish arguments and every pretension that sets itself up against the knowledge of God, and we take captive every thought to make it obedient to Christ" (2 Corinthians 10:4–5). Paul had learned that he could call upon God's power to help destroy strongholds—or habits and inclinations of the flesh—in order to control his thought life. He did this by demolishing excuses and lies that his mind would hurl at him each time it wanted to justify sins of the body.

The apostle Peter also knew how to call upon God's power to overcome temptations of the flesh: "His divine power has given us everything we need for life and godliness through our knowledge of him who called us by his own glory and goodness. Through these he has given us his very great and precious promises, so that through them you may participate in the divine nature and escape the corruption in the world caused by evil desires" (2 Peter 1:3–4). It is obvious that Peter had committed the promises of God to memory in order to use them to battle evil desires. The psalmist cried, "Thy word have I hid in mine heart, that I might not sin against thee" (Psalm 119:11, KJV).

But our obedience to God must go far beyond the suppression of sins of the flesh, which are basically addressed in the Ten Commandments given to Moses. Jesus came to fulfill the law in a new and more positive way. Instead of speaking of what a person should not do, Jesus continually focused on what we should be doing in order to please God. He told us to love our enemies and to do good to those who take advantage of us.

Most of the words in Matthew 23 are the record of a scathing rebuke given by Jesus to the teachers of the law and the Pharisees concerning their hypocrisy. First, Jesus gave this command to his followers: "do not do what they do, for they do not practice what they preach" (Matthew 23:3). To the scribes and Pharisees, Jesus summed up his major complaint against them by stating, "you fast—but you have neglected the more important matters of the law—justice, mercy and faithfulness" (Matthew 23:23).

Common sense would tell us that the Gospel accounts only provide a small sampling of the actual words spoken by Jesus during his three years of ministry. I would be very surprised if Jesus did not at some time remind the Pharisees of words penned by the prophet Isaiah on this subject of true obedience: "Is not this the kind of fasting I have chosen: to loose the chains of injustice and untie the cords of the yoke, to set the oppressed free and break every yoke? Is it not to share your food with the hungry and to provide the poor wanderer with shelter—when you see the naked, to clothe him, and not to turn away from your own flesh and blood? Then your light will break forth like the dawn, and your healing will quickly appear; then your righteousness will go before you, and the glory of the Lord will be your rear guard. Then you will call, and the Lord will answer; you will cry for help, and he will say: Here am I. If you do away with the yoke of oppression, with the pointing finger and malicious talk, and if you spend yourselves in behalf of the hungry and satisfy the needs of the oppressed, then your light will rise in the darkness, and your night will become like the noonday. The Lord will guide you always;

he will satisfy your needs in a sun-scorched land and will strengthen your frame. You will be like a well-watered garden, like a spring whose waters never fail" (Isaiah 58:6–11).

These words of Isaiah are like a breath of fresh air or a cold cup of water to those who are passing through difficult times such as unemployment—those who are trying to discover where God is in their time of confusion. If ever I was asked to state a précis, or brief summary of all of the teaching of Jesus, I think I would begin with these words from Isaiah. Jesus taught consistently that there is a direct link between our acts of justice and God's provision, between our deeds of mercy and God's blessings, between our faithfulness to his Word and his direction for our lives.

A few years ago, as I was involved in renovations to our home, I had occasion to use a plumb line and measuring tape. One day as I picked up the plumb line, I was reminded that the Bible spoke somewhere about God himself owning a plumb line. That night, I looked up the words of Isaiah 28:17: "I will make justice the measuring line and righteousness the plumb line." God was speaking through the prophet concerning his coming judgment of his people. I was then reminded of one of my favorite scriptures, found in Psalm 85:10–13: "Love and faithfulness meet together; righteousness and peace kiss each other. Faithfulness springs forth from the earth, and righteousness looks down from heaven. The Lord will indeed give what is good, and our land will yield its harvest. *Righteousness goes before him and prepares the way for his steps"* (emphasis added).

Later in the book of Isaiah, the prophet reveals another set of measurements used to determine the status of the disobedient: "the measuring line of chaos and the plumb line of desolation" (Isaiah 34:11). I will leave it up to the reader to ponder the significance of that verse. For now, let us focus on what God said to his followers. I believe that if we had no other verse to encourage us to be obedient to God, it would be sufficient to know that "righteousness goes before him and prepares the way for his steps." As our faithfulness rises to God, his righteousness becomes our righteousness, paid for by the sacrifice of Jesus. This fact is fundamental to all teaching of the Bible. If we really want God to lead our steps, then we must be willing to be faithful to his Word. It is as simple as that!

To the Colossian church, Paul wrote, "we pray this in order that you may live a life worthy of the Lord and may please him in every way: bearing fruit in every good work, growing in the knowledge of God, being strengthened with all power according to his glorious might" (Colossians 1:10–11).

Do I have a hunger for God's Word? Do I thirst for his righteousness? Am I willing to "take captive every thought to make it obedient to Christ?" Are my thoughts and actions motivated by justice and mercy? Those are the ingredients of true obedience to God.

Am I obedient?

Life Application—Am I Obedient?

Let these verses help you in your self-evaluation:

Deuteronomy 30:14

Luke 11:28

John 15:10

1 John 3:21–22

2 John 1:6

F. Meek

According to Proverbs 6, God hates a false witness who pours out lies (Proverbs 6:19a), but Jesus said, "Blessed are the meek, for they shall inherit the earth" (Matthew 5:5). The little child who stood before Jesus made no attempt to act grown-up or important—the thought probably never crossed his or her mind. Children don't mind the fact that they sometimes make mistakes or that they are coming across as less than perfect. On the other hand, we adults go to great lengths to hide our imperfections, and we will sometimes do or say anything necessary to convince others that we are cool. Thus we become false witnesses to those around us, pretending to be something that we are not.

Worse than that, our nature is prone to gossip—and even slander, at times—often for the purpose of making ourselves look good. When another person offends us, our first impulse is to run to tell everyone except the offender. We may even embellish the story a bit in order to gain sympathy. If we see or hear of another person who is sinning, we can't wait to tell others about it. Jesus taught that in these situations, rather than telling everyone else, we should go to that person in order to become reconciled in the case of an offence or to bring about correction in the case of sin (Matthew18:15; Luke 17:13).

In John 1, we read about Philip bringing Nathanael to meet the Lord. When Jesus saw Nathanael coming, he said, "Behold an Israelite indeed, in whom is no guile!" (John 1:47, KJV). The NIV reads, "in whom there is nothing false." Although the word *guile* is not used frequently today, the original Greek word means "wily, crafty, or deceitful." Jesus was saying, in effect, that Nathanael was the kind of person who would never consider being a false witness—either about himself or another person.

Unfortunately, our society has developed a somewhat distorted view of what it means to be meek of spirit. The fact that meekness happens to rhyme with weakness does not imply that they mean the same thing. On the contrary, the truly meek person is anything but weak. My dictionary defines the word meek as meaning "showing patience and humility; long-suffering." A truly meek person will not be always seeking his or her own good reputation by putting others down, but will demonstrate patience and understanding with those who sin or offend in order to help that person. Meekness is closely related to humility, and it is difficult (or maybe impossible) to experience one without the other. The difference is that humility looks inward and affects one's attitude toward themselves, whereas meekness looks outward, influencing one's attitude and their interaction with others.

The religious opponents of Jesus recognized his meekness when they came to him and said; "we know you are a man of integrity and that you teach the way of God in accordance with the truth. You aren't swayed by men, because you pay no attention to who they are" (Matthew 22:16b). The truly meek person will never allow a person's wealth or social position to have an influence on their relationship with that person. Jesus showed compassion for everyone who came to him for help, regardless of his or her standing in the community.

It is this genuine concern for others that constitutes the true strength of meekness along with the full knowledge and assurance that each situation we face is another opportunity to demonstrate God's love and grace. Meek people recognize that God is fully on their side and that he may require that they be willing to become "fools for Christ" (1 Corinthians 4:10) in order to bring about his purpose for others. Even when we come under attack by those who would oppose us, we need to keep in mind Paul's words: "Do not take revenge, my friends, but leave room for God's wrath, for it is written: 'It is mine to avenge; I will repay,' says the Lord" (Romans 12:19). On one occasion, I asked God to show me exactly what his word meant by the phrase "leave room for God's wrath." Immediately, I saw in my spirit a picture of a freight train bearing down on me, and heard in my spirit the words "get out of the way!" Even God has a sense of humor.

Just like the other upside-down aspects of God's dealing with people, our strength is demonstrated by our total submission to the will of God for our lives. While it is true that Jesus was "led like a lamb to the slaughter" (Isaiah 53:7) at Calvary, that was a sign of anything but weakness. Jesus said, "No one takes it [my life] from me, but I lay it down of my own accord. I have authority to lay it down and authority to take it up again. This command I received from my Father" (John 10:18).

Patience, humility, a long-suffering spirit, and obedience to God: these are the hallmarks of the truly meek person. Just like humility, the ability to demonstrate meekness will cause people to be attracted to us because of our willingness to listen to others and our unwillingness to pass hasty judgment on those who don't think exactly as we do.

Jesus said the meek shall inherit the earth. If you really want to experience a bit of heaven on earth, try a little meekness.

Am I meek?

Life Application—Am I Meek?

Let these verses help you in your self-evaluation:

Psalm 37:11

Proverbs 19:11

Ephesians 4:2

Colossians 1:10–12

Colossians 3:12

James 5:7

G. Peacemaker

There is something about a small child that can cause men and women to forget their petty differences and offences. Close relatives who gather around the hospital bed of a seriously ill child may have been avoiding each other for years, but suddenly, the possibility of human tragedy involving their own flesh and blood overrides past offences. Perhaps it is because of the child's inability to offend or insult anyone that they are often effective in restoring peace in an otherwise troubled family.

Proverbs 6:19 states that "God hates a man who stirs up dissention among brothers." We live in a world that is marred by discrimination, intolerance, division, and strife. We live in world that is starving for peace. Conflict appears everywhere— between people from different racial backgrounds, between people of different political views, between unions and employers, between religions and people within those religions, between husbands and wives, brothers and sisters, parents and children. According to God's Word, the only reliable source of peace comes through knowledge of and a personal relationship with the Prince of Peace, the Lord Jesus Christ. He alone can calm the troubled waters. He is the only one who has power to turn back the storms in our lives.

Despite all of our anti-discrimination laws, human rights declarations, and codes of ethics, unfair practices appear to be on the increase. It is unfortunate that racial and political acts of intolerance grab all of the newspaper headlines, for there is another very destructive form of strife that can make life unbearable for anyone, anywhere in the world. Millions of people around the world will go to bed weeping and distraught tonight, victims of a largely hidden form of discrimination. Some will turn to substance abuse to try to ease the pain. Others will simply run away, either physically or emotionally. A few will use the ultimate escape and commit suicide because of it. I am talking about emotional abuse motivated by unmet and often unrealistic expectations.

For some reason, this problem is particularly prevalent in family circles, although the workplace may run a close second. The most frequent weapons of this warfare are words, ranging all the way from hurtful criticism to more serious intimidation and threats.

"What causes fights and quarrels among you? Don't they come from your desires that battle within you? You want something but don't get it. You kill and covet, but you cannot have what you want. You quarrel and fight" (James 4:1–2a).

Jesus said, "Blessed are the peacemakers, for they will be called the sons of God" (Matthew 5:9). Very few people reading these words will be sent to a foreign nation to work as a peacekeeper. Not many will be involved in diplomatic services where there is opportunity to influence world peace. But all of us know of families that are being tormented by internal strife and division. According to James, they "want something but don't get it," and so they quarrel and fight, victimizing the very people they care for the most. Paul wrote that this happens because of our sinful nature: "The acts of the sinful nature are obvious—discord, jealousy, fits of rage, selfish ambition, dissensions, factions and envy—and the like. I warn you—those who live like this will not inherit the kingdom of God" (Galatians 5:19–21).

To the young Timothy, Paul wrote, "Do not have anything to do with foolish and stupid arguments, because you know they produce quarrels. And the Lord's servant must not quarrel; instead, he must be kind to everyone, able to teach, not resentful. Those who oppose him he must gently instruct, in the hope that God will grant them repentance leading them to a knowledge of the truth" (2 Timothy 2:23–25).

The writer to the Hebrews used even stronger language on this subject: "Make every effort to live in peace with all men and to be holy; without holiness no one will see the Lord. See to it that no one misses the grace of God and that no bitter root grows up to cause trouble and defile many" (Hebrews 12:14–15).

Ever since Satan was cast down to earth because of his pride and arrogance (Isaiah 14:12), the world has been a literal battleground for the souls of mankind. Because of original sin of Adam and Eve (Genesis 3:1–7), humankind was banished from the Garden of Eden. Now, because of the shed blood of Jesus and his resurrection, people have regained access to peace with God and the means whereby Satan can be defeated. Those who have received peace with God are called to be local distributors of that peace to all around them. "All this is from God, who reconciled us to himself through Christ and gave us the ministry of reconciliation: that God was reconciling the world to himself in Christ, not counting men's sins against them. And he has committed to us the message of reconciliation" (2 Corinthians 5:18).

Note that Paul states we are only committed to *carry the message* of reconciliation. We are not the reconcilers, but simply the messengers, showing and telling others our testimony of Jesus bringing peace into our lives. It is God who reconciles. We can only be effective in leading others toward peace if they can see and feel the peace of God at work in us.

As I searched the Word of God to understand the true meaning of the word *peacemaker,* I was increasingly reminded that, in order to really succeed in making peace, we need all of the other six attributes of a childlike nature. It is as if the Holy Spirit saved peacemaking until last, knowing that it would be impossible to attain without first having a measure of humility, meekness, forgiveness, tenderheartedness, truthfulness, and obedience.

- Humility will demonstrate a visible lack of self-interest, self-promotion, or self-gain so that others will trust our motives and listen to our words.
- Truthfulness will bring credibility and trustworthiness to our testimony, and our

knowledge of God's truth will bring discernment to expose and combat manipulative spirits that seek to create doubt and division.

- Mercy and forgiveness will enable us to avoid condemning others and will make the restoration of relationships possible. Without mercy, we become mere peacekeepers instead of peacemakers.
- A tender heart will allow us to show gentleness, understanding, and compassion, enabling us to follow Paul's advice to be "kind to everyone, able to teach, not resentful" (2 Timothy 2:24).
- Obedience will create in us a testimony of right living, personal integrity, and character. These things are absolutely essential for having the ear of God when we pray for peace. David wrote, "if I had cherished sin in my heart, the Lord would not have listened" (Psalm 66:18).
- Meekness will allow patience, longsuffering, and total dependence on God's wisdom.

"But the wisdom that comes from heaven is first of all pure; then peace-loving, considerate, submissive, full of mercy and good fruit, impartial and sincere. Peacemakers who sow in peace raise a harvest of righteousness" (James 3:17–18).

Jesus is the One who said, "Peace I leave with you; my peace I give you. I do not give to you as the world gives. Do not let your hearts be troubled and do not be afraid" (John 14:27). Just before he returned to sit at the right hand of the Father, Jesus proclaimed, "I have told you these things, so that in me you may have peace. In this world you will have trouble. But take heart! I have overcome the world" (John 16:33). "Let us therefore make every effort to do what leads to peace and to mutual edification" (Romans 14:19).

Am I a peacemaker?

Life Application—Am I a Peacemaker?

Let these verses help you in your self-evaluation:

2 Timothy 2:23–26

James 3:17–18

Proverbs 12:20

Proverbs 14:30

Isaiah 32:17

Isaiah 52:7

Chapter 6—WHAT MUST WE DO?

How did you compare to the greatest in the kingdom? Let me repeat that there is no passing or failure involved in this self-examination. God has given us a pattern to follow in his Son, but he is not looking for people who are perfect. Rather, he desires fellowship with people who would dare to be real, who recognize their imperfections, and who are willing to become more like Jesus through an ongoing process.

The sixth chapter of the Gospel of John is an incredible account of two miracles performed by Jesus and the resulting struggle in the minds of his followers to come to grips with the events of the day. After feeding five thousand people with only five loaves and two fish on a hillside somewhere near Tiberius, the Lord directed his disciples to take their boat and return to Capernaum while he went up into a mountain to pray. Jesus then rejoined the disciples by walking three and one-half miles across the water. Realizing that Jesus had stayed behind but unable to find him, the crowd went in search of him.

According to John's account, when they found Jesus on the other side of the lake, they asked him, "Rabbi, when did you get here?" Jesus answered, "I tell you the truth, you are looking for me, not because you saw miraculous signs but because you ate the loaves and had your fill. Do not work for food that spoils, but for food that endures to eternal life, which the Son of Man will give you. On him God the Father has placed his seal of approval." Then they asked him, *"What must we do to do the works God requires?"* Jesus answered, *"The work of God is this: to believe in the one he has sent "* (John 6:25–29, emphasis added). Minutes later, Jesus declared, "I am the bread of life. He who comes to me will never go hungry, and he who believes in me will never be thirsty" (John 6:35).

What must *we* do to do the work God requires? That same question still begs an answer from people everywhere who are seeking the will of the Father. If we are going to follow the teaching of Jesus in this present-day job search, what would Jesus say to us? Would he also say to us, "Believe in the one he has sent"?

The Bible says that "Jesus Christ is the same yesterday and today and forever" (Hebrews 13:8). The words that he spoke to people of the first century are the same words he would give to us today. The teachings of Jesus are simple and direct. I believe that his sermon to today's unemployed would be a four-part message under the following headings: ask, seek, knock, and give.

Jesus said, "Ask and it will be given to you; seek and you will find; knock and the door will be opened to you. For everyone who asks receives; he who seeks finds; and to him who knocks, the door will be opened" (Matthew 7:7–8). He also said, "Give, and it will be given to you. A good measure, pressed down, shaken together and running over, will be poured into your lap. For with the measure you use, it will be measured to you" (Luke 6:38). For those who seek to do the will of God, these four commands of Jesus still represent the keys to success.

Ask

Believe it or not, some people are almost afraid to ask God for anything. On the other hand, some people are always asking God for everything. Our approach to asking is probably influenced greatly by our perception of the father figure in our own lives—our biological father. Perhaps that is why Jesus included these words: "Which of you, if his son asks for bread, will give him a stone? Or if he asks for a fish, will give him a snake? If you, then, though you are evil, know how to give good gifts to your children, how much more will your Father in heaven give good gifts to those who ask him!" (Matthew 7:9–11). We should never feel reluctant to ask God to meet our needs. In the previous chapter of Matthew, Jesus had said, "your Father knows what you need before you ask him" (Matthew 6:8).

Jesus was directing us to pray. Ever since the days of Abraham, prayer has been a very crucial component of faith in God. Even Adam talked to God, and God talked to Adam. Prayer has never been presented as a one-way monologue, but always as a two-way dialogue with God. As we bring our needs and petitions before God in prayer, he answers in many ways—through his still, small voice within us (sometimes called our conscience), through his Word, through pastors or other believers, and even through circumstances. A very large part of our spiritual growth is dependent on our increasing ability to hear God's voice in all of these ways.

The Bible contains many examples of how we should approach our prayer life. John wrote, "Dear friends, if our hearts do not condemn us, we have confidence before God and receive from him anything we ask, because we obey his commands and do what pleases him" (1 John 3:21–22). Paul taught that by the simple act of combining our requests with thanksgiving, we could overcome our anxiety and receive the peace of God: "Do not be anxious about anything, but in everything, by prayer and petition, with thanksgiving, present your requests to God. And the peace of God, which transcends all understanding, will guard your hearts and your minds in Christ Jesus" (Philippians 4:6–7). James wrote, "You do not have, because you do not ask God. When you ask, you do not receive, because you ask with wrong motives, that you may spend what you get on your pleasures" (James 4:2b–3). And according to the writer of Hebrews, even Jesus sometimes struggled in prayer. "During the days of Jesus' life on earth, he offered up prayers and petitions with loud cries and tears to the one who could save him from death, and he was heard because of his reverent submission" (Hebrews 5:7).

Bible commentaries remind us that Matthew 7:7 carries with it a sense of continuous asking, continuous seeking, and continuous knocking. Some translations of the Bible have interpreted that verse as "keep on asking, keep on seeking, and keep on knocking." On two separate occasions, Jesus told parables about people who were persistent in their petitions. Both were rewarded on account of their persistence (Luke 11:5–8; Luke 18:1–5).

In the John 16, Jesus was preparing his disciples for the time when he would leave to be with the Father. He said, "In that day you will no longer ask me anything. I tell you the truth, my Father will give you whatever you ask in my name. Until now you have not asked for anything in my name. Ask and you will receive, and your joy will be complete" (John 16:23–24). For years, I used the phrase "in Jesus' name" at the end of prayers without actually realizing why I was doing it, except that Jesus directed his disciples to pray that way. Then some book along the way implied that Jesus had in effect given believers his power of attorney in order that they might come to God with his delegated authority, and I accepted that as reasonable. But that interpretation was wrong.

Names were very significant and meaningful to the Hebrews and their descendents, usually signifying some aspect of the character and significance of the person named. When Jesus asked the disciples to pray in his name, he was telling them to approach the Father in a manner that would be worthy of God's Son and our redeemer, recognizing that we have no righteousness of our own, but only the righteousness of Jesus with which to gain access to God (2 Corinthians 5:21). To the very best of our ability, we should imitate his righteousness. "The prayer of a righteous man is powerful and effective" (James 5:16b).

The Gospels of Matthew and Luke both record how Jesus taught his followers to pray. He told us to pray "your kingdom come, your will be done on earth as it is in heaven" (Matthew 6:10). Remembering that Jesus also said, "the kingdom of God is within you" (Luke 17:21), we can begin to grasp the full meaning of praying in Jesus' name. As we allow God's kingdom to rule in our lives and resolve to live according to his will, we will begin to see a dramatic difference in our prayer life—both in terms of intimacy with the Father and in terms of results.

God has a plan for our lives, but there is a very real possibility that we will never know what that plan is unless we develop our willingness to ask him for direction in every area of our lives. We sell ourselves short when we fail to do that. Paul wrote, "No eye has seen, no ear has heard, no mind has conceived what God has prepared for those who love him—but God has revealed it to us by his Spirit. The Spirit searches all things, even the deep things of God. For who among men knows the thoughts of a man except the man's spirit within him? In the same way no one knows the thoughts of God except the Spirit of God" (1 Corinthians 2:9–11).

Seek

Jesus said, "seek first the Kingdom of God" (Matthew 6:33). Do you remember playing hide-and-seek as a child? All but one of the players would hide, leaving the remaining person to come and seek them out. The word *seek* carries with it the assumption that something or someone is either hidden or lost. Believers in the Old Testament were frequently urged by Scriptures to seek the Lord, and when that search became intensely personal, they were encouraged to seek his face. But I can find no reference to seeking the kingdom of God in the Old Testament. I suppose that is logical, since the king had not yet come to earth.

In contrast, the New Testament makes at least sixty-six references to the kingdom of God. Jesus made many comparisons to show his followers what this Kingdom was like, where it was, and what it would mean to those who received it. He encouraged everyone to seek it.

Jesus said, "And do not set your heart on what you will eat or drink; do not worry about it. For the pagan world runs after all such things, and your Father knows that you need them. *But seek his kingdom, and these things will be given to you as well.* Do not be afraid, little flock, for your Father has been pleased to give you the kingdom" (Luke 12:29–32, emphasis added). Once, having been asked by the Pharisees when the kingdom of God would come, Jesus replied, "The kingdom of God does not come with your careful observation, nor will people say, 'Here it is,' or 'There it is,' *because the kingdom of God is within you*" (Luke 17:20–21, emphasis added).

The question that begs an answer is this: if the kingdom of God is within me, why am I encouraged to seek it? The only logical answer to that question is that it must somehow be hidden. Fortunately, we can find it once we recognize the things that keep it hidden.

When we were born again of the Spirit, the Bible tells us that we received the gift of the indwelling Holy Spirit, and so we became host to part of God's kingdom. Through this event, we become a bit of a walking paradox. While our spiritual self wants to shout from the rooftops to tell others about Jesus, our human nature will resist any and all changes to our normal daily routine.

Seeking the kingdom of God within us will, in many cases, require some housecleaning. We will have to work at combating those elements of pride, dishonesty, unwillingness to forgive, disobedience, unconcern, manipulation, or prejudice which may have dominated our thought life previously. If allowed to remain, these things will cause the Spirit of God to be hidden within us as our minds, wills, and emotions continually attempt to control our actions. If we ever want to experience freedom from sin and see God work through us, we must succeed in releasing God's kingdom within us. But we cannot do this job on our own—we need God's help. As we meditate on the seven characteristics of a child, the Holy Spirit will begin showing us those things that need to be dealt with, and we only have to ask God—in the name of Jesus and in the power of that name—to remove each obstacle. Then it is just a matter of believing in the promises of God to deliver us and set us free.

If this kind of activity is new to you, and you are not sure you can handle it, I would encourage you to seek help from your pastor or a Christian counselor. This process is vital for those people who are anxious to see God work in their lives. Despite the fact that you may be desperate for work and overwhelmed with worry for your family and your future, Jesus would still say, "Seek first his kingdom and his righteousness, and all these things will be given to you as well" (Matthew 6:33). In a spiritual sense, it is a matter of life and death. In relation to finding employment, it can mean the difference between finding any old job and finding the job that God has planned for your life.

We have already looked at Jeremiah 29:11, which says, "'For I know the plans I have for you,' declares the LORD, 'plans to prosper you and not to harm you, plans to give you hope and a future.'" Now take a look at the two verses that follow: "Then you will call upon me and come and pray to me, and I will listen to you. You will seek me and find me when you seek me with all your heart" (Jeremiah 29:12–13).

Knock

At one point in my career with our national employment service, I was given the task of planning and implementing a series of seminars for the unemployed using a program called Creative Job Search Techniques. Designed by the well-known Zig Ziglar, this program walked participants through key areas of knowledge required to become re-employed, such as researching the labor market, job interview techniques, and preparation of a resume. The first session of the program began with an examination of how people find jobs by providing a statistical breakdown of the percentage of people finding work through newspaper ads, use of agencies, letters of application, personal contact, etc. At that time—just as today—the majority of successful job searches were the result of personal contact, which involved knocking on the employers' doors to seek out job opportunities.

Although the doors to employment may have changed somewhat over the past thirty years due to technology, the principle is still the same. Jesus still says to us, "Knock, and the door will be opened to you" (Matthew 7:8). We need to examine which doors will lead us to successful re-employment.

The very first door you should knock on is the one named Jesus, who said, "I am the door: by me if any man enter in, he shall be saved, and shall go in and out, and find pasture" (John 10:9, KJV). The second door should be the door of your church, your pastor, or your small group so you can seek vital prayer support during your time of searching. Other doors might include the following:

- employers
- job advertisements in newspapers and periodicals
- local public libraries (to obtain books on job search techniques)
- job agencies or trade organizations (as applicable to your skills)

- post offices (to mail letters of application and resumes)
- web pages (if you have Internet access)
- Friends, neighbors, and relatives who may hear of job opportunities

As you walk through the steps to re-employment, keep the words of Isaiah fresh in your mind: "Although the Lord gives you the bread of adversity and the water of affliction, your teachers will be hidden no more; with your own eyes you will see them. Whether you turn to the right or to the left, your ears will hear a voice behind you, saying, 'This is the way; walk in it'" (Isaiah 30:20–21). Keep on asking God for his help as you sincerely seek to follow his leading. God is waiting to show himself as strong in your life.

Jesus said, "Knock, and the door will be opened to you." Believe it.

Give

For many new believers, one of the most difficult things to understand is the Bible's teaching on giving. It just does not make sense that a loving God—who, according to the Bible, "owns the cattle on a thousand hills" (Psalm 50:10)—would require his children to give him their money, particularly when they themselves are in need. The truth is, we don't give our money directly to God, but we invest it in ministries that are carrying the Gospel to a lost and hurting world, or we give it directly to those who are living in poverty and need. God is not necessarily impressed with tax receipts, but he is pleased when we show genuine love for other people. Even when we have no money in our wallets, we can still give love and our time to those less fortunate than ourselves. Blessings come and go in many disguises, only one of which is money.

God has ordained—and it is unavoidable, no matter how we attempt to skirt around it— that the measure you give will be the measure you receive. You can pray, you can fast, you can beg, plead, or even try to bargain with God for his blessings. God still says, "Give, and it will be given to you. A good measure, pressed down, shaken together and running over, will be poured into your lap. For with the measure you use, it will be measured to you" (Luke 6:38). This is not a test of faith or spirituality, but it is a call to obedience.

How you give—and how much you give—is a matter between you and God. Paul wrote to the Church at Corinth, "On the first day of every week, each one of you should set aside a sum of money in keeping with his income, saving it up, so that when I come no collections will have to be made" (1 Corinthians 16:2).

The entire Gospel is all about giving. God gave his Son. Jesus gave his life. The Holy Spirit gives gifts—comfort and direction. God's angels give protection. God's Word gives faith and hope. And God asks his children to give. An old farmer put it this way: "I shovel it out to the Lord, and he shovels it back. The best thing is that his shovel is much bigger than mine!"

Four short words—ask, seek, knock, and give. Like the small keys that open the doors to our homes, offices, factories, and warehouses, these small but powerful words can unlock the doors to the abundant life that Jesus spoke about. From God's perspective, if we practice those four basic activities faithfully and regularly, we will discover that we are …

Growing Up in Jesus

God's overriding ambition for his children is that we might grow up in our salvation (1 Peter 2:2), and grow up in our relationship with Jesus (Ephesians 4:15). Unfortunately, to those who have not received God's upside-down way of thinking, we will appear to be growing down. James said it clearly: "Humble yourselves before the Lord, and he will lift you up" (James 4:10). Paul wrote, "But God chose the foolish things of the world to shame the wise; God chose the weak things of the world to shame the strong. He chose the lowly things of this world and the despised things—and the things that are not—to nullify the things that are, so that no one may boast before him" (1Corinthians 1:26–29).

We don't need special education, talent, or aptitude to achieve greatness in God's eyes. Someone has said that not many of us will accomplish great things in our lifetime, but all of us are capable of achieving small things in a great way. If every believer did just that, together we would accomplish fantastic things for God's kingdom. As we look forward to our own future with Jesus, it is reassuring to think of his words, recorded twice in Matthew: "But many who are first will be last, and many who are last will be first" (Matthew19:30). "So the last will be first, and the first will be last" (Matthew20:16).

Those two statements form a pair of bookends for the parable of the workers in the vineyard, which was a focal point in the first chapter of this study. In that parable, Jesus taught that God's rewards are not determined by a seniority list or by a time clock. Those who worked for one hour received the same pay as those who worked all day. Jesus emphasized over and over in his teaching that God is more interested in the attitudes of our hearts than in outward appearance, position, or even our production. Those who began working in the first hour of the day found it relatively easy to obtain work, and they could labor all day in the knowledge and assurance that they would be rewarded for their toil at the end of the day. However, those who were hired last had spent a discouraging day traveling from marketplace to marketplace in search of employment—not even giving up when the sundial reached the eleventh hour. Even when the most they could expect would be one hour's wages, they persisted in their search, and they were rewarded for their diligence. God sees and knows our hearts, and rewards accordingly.

This is the bottom line of the gospel: *It is never too late to come to Jesus!* No matter how many times we may have refused to make him Lord of our lives or how many times we run away from him, he still stands at the door of our hearts and wants to come in. Nothing we can do will ever cause him to stop loving us!

Pressing On Toward the Goal

God has a plan for our lives—a plan to prosper us with his brand of riches in order to lead us to success in this life. Just like a human father, God wants to influence our *growing up* in him to train us and prepare us for our destiny. His guidance and direction will begin the moment that we trust in him. Just like a human father, he will lead us one step at a time toward his ultimate goal. Our part is to be sensitive to his leading and open to the genuine desires that he will place in our hearts. With Paul, we need to say "Forgetting what is behind and straining toward what is ahead, I press on toward the goal to win the prize for which God has called me heavenward in Christ Jesus" (Philippians 3:13b-14).

Our heavenly Father knows our every need and has made provision through his Word to meet those needs as we press on toward our goal. He has provided his Holy Spirit to be our companion, our guide, and our comforter in every kind of trouble. He has promised to give us hope—even when things seem hopeless—if we will only commit our hearts to his Son, Jesus. He has made provision for us to receive his riches of wisdom, understanding, and knowledge so we might be equipped to cope successfully with every life situation. Through his Holy Spirit, God promises to enable his children to experience a supernatural power to overcome situations that seem impossible to the human mind.

Sometimes God will allow his children to go through difficult times so they might lean more fully on him and pay heed to his Word. He promised that he would place his desires in our hearts if only we would delight in him, trust him, and commit our ways to him. Through serious study of God's Word, we experience ever-increasing faith that will lead us to the work that God has planned for our lives. Through his Word, we experience a heightened level of love toward others that allows us to be more effective in everything we do. And through his Word, we can realize a new level of hope that enables us to face difficulty—and even persecution—without fear.

Through his Word, God shows us how to live in order to be happy and successful. Using the example of a young child, Jesus taught that our childlike humility will open the way to becoming the kind of person that God desires—the kind of person that the world desperately needs. And by showing us a brief glimpse of life beyond the veil of death, God has helped us to realize that the rewards of obedience to his Word are eternal and everlasting.

What a mighty God we serve!

Life Application—Chapter 6

1. In the first eight verses of Peter's second letter, we have a detailed business plan for claiming and receiving the "very great and precious promises" of Jesus. Read 2 Peter 1:3–8, keeping in mind that Peter's focus was not on achieving material success, but rather on the much greater goal of participating in the divine nature of the Lord. He gives us a complete list of the qualities that will make us effective in our Christian walk (2 Peter 1:8). Underline them, memorize them, and make them a central part of your list of spiritual goals for life. You will not be disappointed!

2. Listed below are some of the Old and New Testament promises that can help when we are facing difficulties such as unemployment—when we are in need of God's provision. Each promise comes with a condition to be met—and a result, a condition to be expected. Read each verse carefully, and record both the condition and the promised result. If possible, memorize as many of the verses as you can, claiming them verbally as you pray. Many people find this method of praying the scriptures to be powerful and effective in building faith and hope.

Verse	Conditon	Promise
Deuteronomy 4:39–40		
Joshua 1:8–9		

Verse	Conditon	Promise
2 Chronicles 7:14		
Isaiah 54:17		
Isaiah 55:6–7		
Isaiah 59:20–21		
Psalm 97:10		
Matthew 18:19–20		
Matthew 21:22		
Mark 11:23–24		
John 14:12–14		
John 15:7		

Verse	Conditon	Promise
John 16:23–24		
2 Corinthians 9:6–8		
1 Thessalonians 4:11–12		
James 1:2–4		
James 1:12		
1 John 3:21–22		
1 John 5:14–15		

Appendix 1—Recommended Further Reading:

Over the past fifty years, I have reviewed many books designed to help people become re-employed. I can honestly say that I have not seen one that I would not recommend to the serious job seeker.

One book, however, stands head and shoulders over all the rest—*What Color Is Your Parachute? A Practical Manual for Job-Hunters and Career-Changers* by Richard Nelson Boles.

If you could have only one book to guide you in your search for employment, this is the book you should buy, for a number of good reasons:

- Although many years have passed since the first self-published edition, author Richard N. Bolles produces an updated edition each year, keeping his advice fresh and relevant to the current labor market.
- This book is written somewhat like a *Reader's Digest,* allowing the reader to pick and choose topics of immediate interest or need.
- Authored by an ordained man of the cloth who himself was thrust into the labor market due to budget cuts, the book includes an epilogue entitled, "How To Find Your Mission In Life— God and One's Vocation."

Appendix 2—Readers Feedback Requested

Do you have a testimony to share with others concerning the way in which God has met your need for suitable employment? Your testimony can be an inspiration and help to others who are unemployed. Please send a brief summary of your story to the author. God willing, selected entries will be published in a book of encouragement.

Suggested Format

Name:
Address:
Phone Number:
E-mail Address:
Occupation:
Date Submitted:
Brief details of Testimony (200 words or fewer, please):

All submissions will be acknowledged wherever possible. Selected respondents will be contacted for more details and verification. Testimonies will NOT be printed without approval of final text by the respondent.

Please E-mail your testimonies to
wayne@bwaynebradfield.com